Skues on Trout

George Edward Mackenzie Skues, illustration by Marsha Karle

Skues on Trout

OBSERVATIONS FROM
AN ANGLER NATURALIST

*Selected and introduced
by Paul Schullery*

STACKPOLE
BOOKS

Published by
STACKPOLE BOOKS
5067 Ritter Road
Mechanicsburg, PA 17055
www.stackpolebooks.com

Printed in the United States

First edition

10 9 8 7 6 5 4 3 2 1

Library of Congress Cataloging-in-Publication Data

Skues, G. E. M. (George Edward Mackenzie)
  Skues on trout: observations from an angler naturalist /
selected and introduced by Paul Schullery.—1st ed.
     p. cm.
  ISBN-13: 978-0-8117-0358-1 (hardcover)
  ISBN-10: 0-8117-0358-4 (hardcover)
  1. Trout fishing—Anecdotes. 2. Fly fishing—Anecdotes.
3. Skues, G. E. M. (George Edward Mackenzie) I. Schullery,
Paul. II. Title.

SH687.S447 2008
799. 17'57—dc22

                                              2007036713

SERIES INTRODUCTION

We fly fishers are rightly proud of our long and distinguished literary tradition, but too much of that tradition has slipped out of reach. It is unfortunate enough that most of the older books are unobtainable, but as the sport's techniques, language, and even values change, the older authors become less accessible to us even when we do read them. Fly fishing's great old stories and wisdoms are often concealed in unfamiliar prose styles, extinct tackle terminology, and abandoned jargon.

The lessons and excitement of these older works will only survive if we keep reading them. By presenting the most readily accessible material from these authors, this series invites you to explore the rest of their work. Whether the selections in each book are instructive, entertaining, or inspirational, it is our fondest hope that they will whet your appetite for more of this lovely sport's literary adventures.

It is one of fly fishing's greatest attractions that the actual fishing is accompanied by a vast and endlessly engaging conversation. We have been conducting this conversation in print for many centuries now, and we seem always to have more to say. In this series, we invite you to sit back, turn the page, and give a listen. The conversation has never been better.

Paul Schullery
Series editor

CONTENTS

PART III: *The Vision of Trout continued*

PART IV: *How*   **70**

Contents

INTRODUCTION

The British angling writer George Edward
Mackenzie Skues (1858–1949) has been
described not only as the father of nymph fishing,
but as the greatest fly fisher who ever lived. He was
also a modest, humorous, and warmly accessible
writer whose writings never lost sympathy for his fel-
low anglers. His self-deprecating and deceptively
simple-sounding writings on trout and fly fishing
remain among the wisest and most revealing in the
sport's enormous literature.

I came to my interest in fishing literature from
voluminous reading in a parallel literary universe,
that of natural history. With that perspective I am
convinced that had Skues chosen to devote his
energy, observational gifts, and literary skill to almost
any element of the natural scene other than fish, he

would have achieved far broader public renown than he did in the relatively narrow readership of fly fishing. He was a great nature writer.

That said, Skues's initial fame in fly fishing came about in good part because he led the way in correcting the excesses of the "dry-fly revolution" that Frederic Halford and his colleagues launched on the southern British chalk streams in closing decades of the 1800s. Halford, whose dry-fly teachings were showcased in *Halford on the Dry Fly*, one of the inaugural volumes in this series, symbolized a movement in angling that, for all its wise theorizing and scientific precision, soon approached bigotry in its condescension toward other fly-fishing methods. It is difficult for us today, accustomed to a happy diversity of fly-fishing methods and tastes, to imagine the intensity of the dry-fly specialist's self-pronounced superiority a hundred years ago. But such was the atmosphere in which Skues learned to fish, and against which he so effectively reacted in his own writings.

Skues's first book, *Minor Tactics of the Chalk Stream* (1910), tentatively rebelled against the exclusivity with which dry-fly advocates perceived themselves as the highest and most refined form of anglers. His second book, which many still regard as his masterpiece, was *The Way of a Trout with a Fly* (1921), and it quickly established him as one of the day's great angling theorists—as it also established the intellectual and ethical basis for sunken flies as legitimate tools of a well-rounded angler.

But it would be a great disservice to Skues to regard him merely as an iconoclast whose only legacy is that he saved fly fishing from its own worst impulses. He did not base his fly-fishing theories on a blind devotion to the older wet-fly styles that had preceded the Halford era. Instead, he built on the older traditions of sunk flies as effective imitations of immature forms of insects while employing key elements of the dry-fly specialist's methods.

He advanced this corrective process with remarkable speed. Colonel E. W. Harding, another of the twentieth century's most thoughtful angler-naturalists, was among those offended by the "arrogance" of the "cult of the dry fly." As early as 1931, he said that Skues "restored balance and tolerant sanity to the sport" because he "extended the dry fly purists' technique to the use of the wet fly and created a new and delicate branch of the art of fly fishing."

That "branch" is usually known as nymph fishing. And though many generations of anglers had appreciated the value of imitating subaquatic insects, to Skues goes the foremost credit for codifying the theory and practice of this kind of fishing among modern anglers. It is no wonder that Brian Clarke and John Goddard, in their own milestone book, *The Trout and the Fly* (1980), described Skues as "the greatest liberator of the human mind in fly fishing in this century."

For this sampler of Skues's writings, I have chosen to excerpt his pathbreaking study of trout behavior that occupies the first "division" of *The Way of a Trout with a Fly.* I am aware of no other book, and certainly no book published up to Skues's time, that contained anywhere near as perceptive and helpful a study of the creature our sport depends upon. I think of it as brilliant nature writing thinly disguised as a superb fishing book. The already world-famous chalk streams of southern England, with their slow, clear currents and readily observable trout, provided Skues with the perfect laboratory in which to study the behavior of a fish whose daily life had remained a mystery to most anglers for many centuries.

In fact, rereading Skues now I am reminded of the old story about the college sophomore who naively complained that he didn't like to read Shakespeare's plays because they were so full of cliches. There is hard-earned wisdom in our modern understanding of the trout as a fly-fishing quarry, and it's hard to overstate how much of that wisdom was first or best articulated right here.

Naturally, we now know more of some subjects, such as the vision of trout, than Skues did so long ago. But on most topics, we are still holding these same inquiries on the stream as we attend to the descendants of the fish that so engaged and baffled the anglers of Skues's day. Nobody has ever thought harder or more creatively than he did about the questions that vex and intrigue us as anglers, or watched fish with a more penetrating eye, or gave us more charming disquisitions on the whole fly-fishing scene. As I worked on my own recent book about how trout take a fly, *The Rise* (2006), I was repeatedly struck by how often, and how thoughtfully, Skues had plowed the same theoretical ground.

As mentioned in the series introduction, it is our goal to make these new editions of older fishing writings as accessible to the modern reader as possible. My own first encounters with many of the older fly-fishing books were halting and confused by the great changes that have occurred in the language and practice of the sport. Even a hundred-year-old book can be almost impenetrable to the new reader who isn't familiar with the old terms and attitudes. It is to

Skues's credit that there are relatively few such obstacles in the following text—I will mention a few in a moment—but let me first encourage you not to worry much about them. Skues's greater meaning is always clear even if some specific detail is not. Like every specialist of every age, he had his own jargon; some of his fly patterns you may recognize, many you may not. I hope you'll want to learn more about them all later, but for now they aren't as important as the greater story of which they are just a detail. Feel free to read past them for the story's real point.

The modern reader's problems with Skues may mostly involve minor matters of terminology. Depending upon where you fish, you may or may not recognize a "sedge" as a caddisfly (the "grannom" was a type of sedge), though the word is also used to describe some tall water plants. For Skues and his chalkstream companions, the May fly was not any mayfly; it was a certain very large mayfly that occupies a position of significance in the chalkstream angler's year much like the one occupied by the Green Drake in the American East or the "salmon fly" in the American West. On the other end of the size spectrum, the "smut" was some very tiny insect, and trout that were "smutting" were feeding on it. Likewise, a "curse" was an exasperatingly small fly.

Smut, midge, and curse were at times interchangeable terms. Some of his scientific terminology for certain groups of insects has gone by the wayside, but he gives the common names for those groups as well, so you shouldn't get lost there.

A "brace" is a pair. "Gut" was silkworm gut, the translucent fiber extracted from silkworms that was used by almost all anglers for leader material; at first glance it looks like modern monofilament. His mentions of "weed-cutting" refer to the intensive management of aquatic vegetation that was by Skues's time a routine part of chalkstream fishing. You will notice here and there indications that the Test, Itchen, and other streams enjoyed by Skues and his comfortably well-off companions were in many ways engineered specifically for the enhanced enjoyment of their fly-fishing proprietors, to an extent rare on most American public waters. Skues fished in a different world, but a trout is always a trout, and the same challenges and lessons apply now as then when we try to catch one.

Though I encourage you not to let unfamiliar details distract you, I do wish that when you come upon the name of some authority whom Skues invokes you will make a mental note to track down that person's work some day. Halford, Mottram,

Stewart, Ronalds, Younger, and many other very smart fly fishers informed Skues's thinking. Whether you realize it or not, they inform yours, too.

Last there is the matter of Skues's own example as a reader. As you will see, he read voraciously but with a fine eye to the trustworthiness of each book. (Is there a wiser observation on reading than his opening line: "Authorities darken counsel"?) So I suspect that if he could offer you any advice about how to read this little book, he would tell you to read it cautiously. He has already turned out to be wrong in his conviction, so forcefully expressed near the end of the book, that of all the aquatic insects only the mayflies can be successfully imitated in their immature forms. I expect and hope that you will find other things to disagree with, or at least reserve judgment on. Skues knew better than most of us that fly fishing isn't about finding the final answers to our fishing questions; it's about the "bafflement" of trying to understand a creature whose world, though so close to our own, is so utterly and beautifully different.

Paul Schullery

THE WAY OF A TROUT
WITH A FLY

When the Wise Man laid it down that there were three things which were too wonderful for him—yea, four which he knew not—he came to the climax with "the way of a man with a maid." Some future Solomon will end with a fifth—the way of a trout with a fly—for it combines the poise of the eagle in the air, the swift certainty of a serpent upon a rock, and the mystery of the way of a ship in the midst of the sea, with the incalculableness of the way of a man with a maid. Our aviators seem to be on their way towards a solution of the way of the eagle in the air. The mystery of the way of a ship in the midst of the sea has yielded all its secrets to the persistence of modern man, but the way of a man with a maid and the way of a trout with a fly remain with us to be a delight and a torment to thousands of generations yet unborn.

FOREWORD

Authorities darken counsel. An authority is a person engaged in the invidious business of stereotyping and disseminating information, frequently incorrect. Angling literature teems with examples. I imagine that few anglers have devoted more time than I have to the study of authorities. From Dame Juliana to the latest issue of the press there is scarcely a book on trout-fly dressing and trout fishing which I have not studied and analyzed, and this conclusion seems to me inevitable. It was not until I realized this that my reading became any use to me. Up to that point I had been swallowing wholesale, with my facts, all sorts of fallacies and inaccuracies, alike in the matter of dressings and their use, and what they were intended to represent. From that point on an author became merely a suggester of experiment—a means of testing and checking my own observations by the water side, and no longer a small god to be believed in and trusted as infallible. And that is all an author, writing on any progressive art or science, ought to be. It is good now and again to have the ideas and discoveries of an epoch analyzed in the crucible of some acute intellect, and the problem restated, but this age has put an end to all belief in finality, and the business of that analysis should be to clear away the lumber of the past, while preserving all that is of value, and not to add more than can be helped to the lumber that some later writer will strive—probably in vain—to clear away. An authority who lays down a law and dogmatizes is a narcotic, a soporific, a stupefier, an opiate. The true function of an authority is to stimulate, not to paralyze, original thinking. But then, I suppose, he wouldn't be an authority.

Since the very beginning of things men have talked fish and fishing, just as they have talked religion and metaphysics, without progress commensurate with the amount of labour and energy expended, and with as many divergencies to right and left and as much slipping back and floundering in morasses of error. That the subject is so eternally interesting is my only excuse for the collection of the speculations contained in the ensuing pages. That they advance the sum of human knowledge on the subjects with which they deal is too much to hope.

G. E. M. Skues

PART I

I
Considerations of Motive

One frequently sees it maintained in books and in articles in the press that it is impossible to say why trout come on to the rise. With all possible respect for the distinguished authors of those books and articles, I venture to disagree. Trout come on to the rise for two reasons in combination—(1) because they are hungry, and (2) because there is food. It is no answer to say that frequently fly is in quantity on the water and is neglected. That is quite true, and yet it is consistent with the trout not being hungry—being perhaps gorged—or being busy with some preferable diet under water. It is clear that the trout do not rise without something to rise at, that when they come on to the rise they do so with remarkable unanimity, that they leave off with a unanimity almost as remarkable, that when fly food is scarce they do not rise as freely as when it is plentiful. And when it is plentiful and they are not rising it is not too great an assumption to suggest that it is because they are not hungry. It is probably within the experience of most chalk-stream anglers that fleets of upwinged duns sail down neglected, with only a trout rising fitfully here and there among them, and that that trout here and there is singularly amenable to the attraction of an iron-blue dun. That only means that trout have a preference for one food over another and are at times so gorged as to be dainty. After a long course of one insect they are apt to prefer another. In liking a change of diet they do not differ greatly from ourselves. That diet may be sought on the surface, in mid-water, in the weeds, or on the bottom. It is an entire mistake to assume that the trout is only feeding during the rise. It is indeed probable that there are few hours of the day when he is not feeding on something—mainly down below. And if his subaqueous supplies be plentiful and filling it would easily account for his not being excited by a plentiful exhibition of surface food. Indeed, the examples of dour rivers like the lower and middle Kennet and the Middlesex Colne prove that there are cases where the supply of bottom food is so large as to keep the trout down below in the absence of the rare attraction of the May fly or the large red sedge, and at times the grannom. The Kennet at any rate breeds large quantities of duns. The fact that the upper Kennet is less dour only proves that the supply of bottom food is less satisfying. But it is still more satisfying than that of such rivers as the Itchen and the Test and free-rising streams of that class. And there are all degrees of stream in between these two ends of the scale. There is, therefore, no real mystery about the question why trout rise to the fly. The only real problem is why at times, when everything appears in favour of their doing so, they do not. It may, however, be assumed that there is a common-sense reason for it. In nature nothing happens without a reason. The difficulty for the angler is merely that the reason is hidden some way beneath the surface. There may be occasions when trout take the fly for sport or high spirits, jealousy, or curiosity, or some by-motive; but on these occasions it may be taken for granted that the temptation is scarce and that hunger is in abeyance.

II

The Why

The question why the trout takes the artificial fly is another question altogether and deserves a separate examination. Speaking generally, it takes the fly as food. But it may be induced to take it from hunger (deceived by its resemblance to the natural insect), as in the case of the floating fly or the sunken nymph; from hunger (attracted by the motion of a tripped or dragging sunk fly rather than by any close resemblance to a natural insect); from curiosity (attracted by some fancy pattern, such as Wickham's Fancy, or Red Tag); from rapacity (excited by the spectacle of some big dragging fly); from tyranny (induced by the spectacle of something seemingly alive and in distress)—or there may be a combination of some or all of these motives. The angler will, therefore, be wise who considers, in relation to the water it is his privilege to fish, on which of these motives he can most profitably place reliance, and adjusts his methods accordingly. In some waters the fish are generally risers. In others, where the appeal of the fly is more commonly to motives other than hunger, they are strikers. The American angler seldom uses the term "rise." He has "a strike." And it may be believed that the term is just. A book of American trout flies shows a large majority of them to be fancy flies, appealing to curiosity, rapacity, tyranny, or jealousy, rather than to hunger. There are British waters and parts of waters where strikers are more common than risers. For instance, in a slow, almost still, mill-head the trout, moving about on the bottom or at the surface in search of food, will (unless smutting) with difficulty be tempted to take a floating fly, however good an imitation it be of a natural insect, but will without difficulty be lured to slash at a dragging fly, the resemblance of which to a natural insect is not marked. In such a place the angler has often the choice between not catching the fish and applying the appropriate method of the dragging fly. I do not approve of the dragging fly on the open chalk stream, but in the case of such a mill-head I should not hesitate to use it, though confessedly it is, as a method, far less interesting than is the taking of the trout with the genuine imitation or representation or suggestion of the natural fly.

Why does the trout take the natural fly? Undoubtedly, as the contents of his stomach prove, as food. Why does he take the artificial fly? In my opinion, in the vast majority of cases, because he supposes it to be his food. On occasion the motive may be curiosity, jealousy, pugnacity, or sheer excess of high spirits. But if I did not believe that the trout took the artificial fly not only as food but as food of the kind on which he is feeding, the real interest of trout fishing would be gone, so far as I am concerned. That is the reason why, for me, trout fishing on chalk streams transcends in interest any other kind of trout fishing. For on streams where the fly is comparatively scarce trout are more apt to take any kind of insect that may be on the menu, and are to be taken freely on patterns which do not represent the fly on the water. But chalk streams are rich in insect food. The duns come out in droves, and the fish show a discriminating determination to take only one pattern at a time, which convinces me that they mean to have nothing which does not satisfy them as being that on which they are feeding. Even on chalk streams there are occasions when there are exceptions to this rule, but in my experience, stretching over thirty-five years, these occasions are few.

III

Freewill and Predestination

A year or two before the war a learned German Professor, Herr Ludwig Edinger, contributed to the *Field* an article entitled, "Fish and Freewill," in which he sought to prove that it was by an involuntary reflex action that the trout took the fly. "The trout," said he in effect, "is a creature of very little brain." In the higher vertebrates a special portion of the brain—the cortex of the cerebral hemisphere—has alone the function of combining different sensations and of drawing conclusions from them. If deprived of their cortex they exercise no choice, and have no power of deliberation, but react in a definite way to each definite change in their surroundings. "A study of the anatomical and microscopical structure"—I quote his exact words—"of the brain of fish shows that there is no structure corresponding to the cortex in the more highly developed forms." Hence he declared that fish have no power of combining their sensations, and that they cannot exercise choice. So that the action of the trout in taking the fly is purely reflex, depending on two factors—viz., upon the stimulus being adequate and upon the degree of excitability of the nerve centres—and the Professor went on to develop his argument in some detail.

The fly so cunningly cast by the Professor evoked several rises. More than one angler rushed into print with facts confirmatory of the Professor's theory.

I suspect Professor Ludwig Edinger of being a humorist of the most cynical and heartless type. Who that was not could so wrap up a platitude in learned language and spring it upon innocent anglers in such a way as to lead them to think that they were trembling on the verge of a portentous discovery which should knock their dearly loved art into the proverbial cocked-hat? "Has a fish no option when it takes a fly?" "None," says he, "when the temptation is irresistible." Only he does not put it in that nice plain way. He envelops his proposition in a cloud of cortices and reflexes and other fearful wild-fowl; and scared readers rush into print with their evidence, confirmatory or negative. The Professor neatly brought down his game, and must have chuckled in his sleeve. I suggest to him that his next quarry be a theological Congress to whom he might propound similar riddles on the fall of man—and was Eve compelled to eat the apple, and what was the nature of the reflex of which Delilah was the victim which compelled her to keep Samson's hair cut? And were

Eve and Delilah respectively *sans cortex,* or were there only rudimentary cortices in their skulls?

But be reassured. Professor Ludwig Edinger is quite right. The trout has no option when he takes the fly, and it doesn't matter in the least to the art of angling. The art is to present the lure so that it shall be an irresistible temptation. If it isn't so, in the circumstances the trout won't take it. Why is the artificial fly irresistible when he takes it? Because he thinks it is a natural fly and good to eat, or else because it excites his curiosity or bullying propensities. Then the reflex acts. If it doesn't look to him like a natural fly and good to eat, or if it doesn't excite his curiosity or bullying propensities, the reflex does not act, because the stimulus is not there. "That's all there is to it," as they say in the States. So the angler is still faced with the eternal problem, how to provide the stimulus which excites the reflex action, and how to place it so as to excite that action. It is just as difficult to do these things since Professor Edinger flung his epoch-making discovery before an astonished world, and it will probably go on being difficult just so long as trout are trout. The trout, being a slow-witted person and so fashioned by a merciful Providence, is apt to look twice at a solitary specimen of any kind of insect before attacking it. But, given a sufficient supply, he awakes in time to the notion that there is game afoot, and it is probably just the same if the artificial fly be tendered him again and again without a mistake. He may begin to suspect a hatch, and may irresistibly be led to respond to the stimulus. Fortunately there are other stimuli to which he responds with equal inevitability—funk, for instance. So that the fearful may take heart of grace; and may even suspect that, when the learned Professor had had his laugh out at the readiness with which the anglers' reflexes responded to his stimuli, and had settled whether there were any or only rudimentary cortices to their brains, things went on just as they were before, and that they will so continue.

It doesn't matter a bit in the world whether the trout reasons that the artificial fly is unsatisfactory or whether his sensations suggest to him that it is not a fly. In either case the angler won't get him that chuck. It does not matter whether his perceptions or his reason suggests to him that that is a fly and good to eat. Perceptions which lead to logical conclusions are as near a form of reason as is good for the angler, even if the premises or one of them—the fly, to wit—be a wrong 'un.

PART II

I
The Sense of Taste

That trout have some sense of taste can, I think, hardly be doubted. The excitement with which they come on to a rise of iron-blues must indicate that the fly or nymph gives them some special satisfaction. Their greedy devotion to the black gnat, too, and, on occasion, the eagerness with which they take willow fly and alder are evidence of the same kind. They take the artificial fly as food, but are extremely quick to reject it from their mouths, and that is why quick striking is necessary. Probably they have more sense of taste than have chub. I recall casting an artificial Alder to a chub which lay in a still little pool among lily pads. As the fly lit the fish turned and lay at right angles to its former position. I did not strike, as I thought the fish had missed the fly, but I waited some couple of minutes to let the fly and gut sink well below the fish before I attempted to retrieve my cast. But when I did so I found to my astonishment that the fish was hooked. It must have sucked in the fly as it turned, and the fly must have been in its mouth a couple of minutes before my attempt to retrieve it pulled in the barb. If the fish had any appreciable sense of taste it would have ejected the bunch of feather and herl immediately. A trout would certainly have done so.

II

The Sense of Smell

It is equally certain that trout have some sense of smell. They can find their way by it to a place baited with worms even in the thickest water; and in thick water they would probably starve but for the sense of smell. But it may well be doubted whether they place any reliance on it when taking the fly, natural or artificial. Here, one must infer, they are guided entirely by sight. If they relied on smell the paraffin anointment of the artificial dry fly would hardly fail to put them off; and the absence of an insect smell in the case of a wet fly might be expected to warn them to be careful. Insects have, many of them, quite a strong scent. A box of stone-fly creeper is very distinctly odorous.

It is, moreover, well known that a gentle or a caddis worm on the hook of a fly often proves irresistible to a trout, and the fact is made use of by unscrupulous anglers. But here the fish is taking the savoury gentle or caddis worm and not the fly, and it is still true that in taking the fly he depends so much more on vision than on any other sense that for the purposes of fly fishing smell and taste may be disregarded. But the vision of the trout, in its nature and peculiarities, deserves a closer study than it has ever, so far as I know, received.

PART III

The Vision of Trout

I

A Preliminary Cast

In a well-known Greek myth, Semele, one of Jove's many mistresses, is presented as having persuaded her lover to reveal himself to her in his Olympian majesty, and as having been burned to a cinder in the conflagration;—the moral of this being that man is not intended to see things as they are, but only in such form and to such extent as is good for him. This is, I believe, in full accord with the views of modern science, which holds that man sees nothing absolutely as it is, but only relatively and as is necessary for the purposes of his being. Even so his perception of things seen is not the sole result of the image on the retina, but is a subjective effect produced upon the mind by the combination of the image and the results of experience gained through the sense of touch and possibly other senses connecting and coordinating the image thrown upon the retina. A baby, it is supposed, sees everything flat at first. He has to feel his way through his sense of touch to a sense of distance and perspective. Man's eye therefore is not in the absolute sense a perfect organ, but only relatively perfect for the purposes of the needs and nature of man.

I do not think that, if this proposition be true of man, it can be any less true of fish, and, in considering the way of a trout with a fly, whether natural or artificial, it may be worth while to spend a little time in an endeavour to see what can be deduced from known facts about the nature and characteristics of the eyesight of the trout.

The nature and the needs of trout differ greatly from those of man, and it need not therefore surprise us if examination should lead us eventually to the conclusion that his perception by eyesight differs materially from that of man. Indeed, I think it would be remarkable if, living in a different medium that is subject to certain optical laws from which the air is free, and having different needs and modes of being from man, the trout were to see things in all respects as man sees them—even after making all allowance for the correcting and co-ordinating effects of tactile experience.

To begin with, while man's eyes are placed in front of his head and operate together so that his vision is stereoscopic, the trout's eyes are on the sides of his head, slanting slightly forward and operating separately, so that it may be inferred that in most cases his vision of an object is monocular. It may be that in the act of taking a fly, whether on the surface or below it, both eyes may be trained forward upon the object, or, alternatively, that one eye only may be on the object and the other attending to business in another direction.

Then, though the vision of a trout is astonishingly quick, enabling him as it does to pick out and capture minute living objects, often in rapid and turbulent streams, it does not seem to be greatly concerned with a sense of form or detail. Otherwise it is extremely difficult to conceive how he can take a hackled fly, such, for instance, as the Straddlebug May fly, with its long straggling fibres of summer duck, in circumstances which can leave no doubt in any unprejudiced mind that he takes it for May fly or a hatching nymph. In the case of smaller soft-hackled patterns the case is only a shade less wonderful, and even in the cases where the imitation or representation of the natural fly is most lifelike, it cannot be suggested that the likeness is so precise that it could for a moment deceive the eyesight of man.

In the matter of the trout's colour perception there has been much divergence of opinion among anglers. Some have gone so far as to suggest that the trout is colour-blind. Some say he perceives tone only and not colour. Others would have you believe that he sees colour precisely as does man. I am not of the school which would class the trout as colour-blind. I am assured by a man of science who has studied the subject that in the retina of the trout, the seat of colour vision, no differences in quality from that of man are to be found. The same elements are to be found in human beings and in the trout. These are, of course, structural differences. The medium, water, in which the trout lives renders a spherical lens behind a flat cornea necessary. The method of adjustment of focus differs from that of man, the eye of the fish being accommodated for near vision, and the entire retina of the trout's eye appears to be sensitive, instead of merely one spot. But, allowing for these differences of mechanism, there is no obvious or apparent essential difference. And I am asked to infer from this that trout see colour precisely as do men. It

The pathbreaking writings of British dry-fly pioneer Frederic Halford (who often used the pen name "Detached Badger"), came under critical scrutiny from the more open-minded G. E. M. Skues. From Martin Mosely, The Dry-Fly Fisherman's Entomology *(1921).*

may be so. I do not know. But I would ask whether an examination of the retina of a man who is wholly or partially colour-blind shows any differences from the retina of a man of entirely normal vision. If no differences are shown, why may not the trout, notwithstanding his similar retina, be partially colour-blind without the fact being betrayed by his retina? The lines of the spectrum are numerous, and I would ask, is it not conceivable that the trout may have a faculty of perceiving some to which man is insensitive and even some beyond the range of colour visible to man at either or both ends of the spectrum? I do not know, but Nature is so marvellously various and so fertile in expedient that I should hesitate to call it impossible that it should be so. The subject is one which will bear a good deal more thinking over and investigation than it has hitherto received, and I propose to examine it at more length at a later stage.

II

The Sense of Form and Definition

The trout is credited on authority with being the keenest-eyed of animals, and doubtless most of us have too frequently found him keener of sight than we have cared about. Yet the nature and limitations of that keenness are well worth examining if we are to get a working grip of the principle which should underlie the art of trout-fly dressing. In examining the question of the possibility of successfully using imitations of larvae or nymphs for trout fishing, Mr. F. M. Halford, after supposing that the angler has turned out a fairly good imitation of the nymph, and tries it at a time when the fish are bulging incessantly at natural larvae, says:

"Alas! how woefully is he *désillusioné*. The fish will not look at this, although it is an admirable representation, both in colour and shape, of the natural insect. . . . How is it to be expected that a timid, shy fish like a trout, who from painful daily, and even hourly, experience is warned to use the keenest of all the senses with which he has been endowed by nature—viz., his sight for his protection, should mistake that motionless, supine compound of dubbing, silk, quill, and hackle, drifting helplessly and lifelessly like a log down the stream, for the active, ever-moving larva sparkling in the sunshine, and varying in colour at every motion as rays of light strike it at different angles?"

Now, accepting for the sake of argument this presentation of the action and appearance of the larva as correct, we have to reconcile it with the fact that this shy, keen-sighted fish does not infrequently take the artificial fly of the angler, floating, sunken, or semi-submerged, at times and under conditions which can leave no doubt in any reasonable mind that he takes it for the natural fly which it feebly pretends to represent. What is the inevitable conclusion? Undoubtedly that the eyesight of the trout, though perfectly adapted for all his purposes except defence against the wiles of man, is defective in some direction or directions, since it permits him to make such fatal mistakes. But how can we know the nature and extent of these defects in his eyesight? There are two ways of getting at it. One is by microscopic examination of the trout's eye by a skilled oculist or optician—a method beyond me; the other is by reasoning from the innumerable data which a prolonged experience of trout-fly fishing gives to every observant angler.

The first point to which I invite attention is that a trout is a predaceous animal, and his eye may be expected to evince the peculiarities of the eyes of other predaceous animals whose business it is to catch their prey in motion. One naturally turns to the cat for a familiar example. If anyone has watched a cat at play, he may guess to what I am leading up. For a moving object her sight is of amazing quickness, but she is far more stupid than the dog at finding a stationary object, unless guided by the sense of smell. Is this true of the trout? Let us follow the inquiry further. The cat not only sees things in motion, it sees them moving in the dark. The trout also has a faculty for seeing—at any rate in his own element—in the dark, and even distinguishes colour well—quite well enough to enable him to take one artificial fly rather than another. Most anglers who have fished wet-fly streams in the late dusk with a team of flies could quote occasions when one fly has been taken by every fish to the exclusion of a choice of other patterns, and that fly not necessarily either the lightest or the darkest.

Let us grant, then, that the trout's sight is quick; let us concede him a strong sense of colour or texture or both; but is that sight clear? Has the trout even a rudimentary sense of form? There are grounds for doubting it. I am going to get into hot water with the apostles of the "precise imitation" school, but I am not going to dogmatize, but to call attention to facts.

If we take the most exquisitely dressed Olive Quill or Iron-blue dun and compare them with their prototypes in nature, can we honestly say that the resemblance of form or attitude is marked? We know it is not. We are satisfied if in colour and size the imitation is approximate. If the fly be tied with rolled wings reversed, it is frequently as good a killer as, or even better than, the ordinary pattern. Yet the fly with dense, stiff wings thrown forward is really not, in shape at any rate, a striking likeness of the natural insect, with its wings sloping just the other way. A good instance of this is the Mole Fly—a sedge;

instead of having its wings laid back over the body, it presents them flung forward in the opposite direction. Yet it is indubitably a successful pattern. Then, does the trout pay much attention to the fact that the floating fly of commerce is generally able to give the centipede fifty legs and a beating? There are times when he does not. Does he even mind where the legs occur in the anatomy (if one may be pardoned the term) of the artificial fly? They may, as in the Wickham or any of the sedges, be in spirals all down the body, but what does he care? Take the Dotterel dun. This is a hackled imitation of a light yellow-legged dun. The dotterel hackle is a brownish dun feather with yellow tips to the points of the fibres. The dun colour represents the wings, the yellow tips the legs. But does the trout resent being offered a fly with yellow legs at the tips of his wings, and these wings spread mopwise all round his body? If he does resent it, the popularity—the well-deserved popularity—of the Dotterel dun is hard to account for. Making every allowance for some disarrangement of toilet in a natural fly which has become submerged or caught by the current, can we say that it ever has its wings starred all round its head or shoulders in a palpitating mop? Then the honey-dun hen hackle. This is the same thing again. And we know that the honey-dun hen feathers are among the trout-fly dresser's most cherished treasures.

Let us turn to the Iron-blue dun. The natural insect has lead-coloured wings and red feet, and the artificial may be dressed either winged or hackled. If hackled, a dark blue dun feather with copper-red points is an admirable feather to use. But the trout does not mind a bit that your Iron-blue dun has a mop of blue wing all round its head, with a little red foot at the end of each fibre. It is a commonplace of fly dressing that, in translating a winged pattern into its hackled correlative, you select a hackle combining as far as possible the colour of wings and legs, and, so long as you keep the colours, their relative position is of little consequence. As an instance, let me quote the case of the Lead-winged (*i.e.,* starling-winged) Coachman and the Little Chap. Each has a peacock herl body. The dun of the starling wings in the Coachman is reproduced by the dun centre of the hackle of the Little Chap, and the red hackle of the Coachman by the red points of the hackle of the Little Chap. But if they be dressed on the same size of hook, when one will kill, as a general proposition the other will kill. If the artificial fly lay on quite still water it may be doubted whether it would often be taken; but in general the movement of the stream imparts an appearance of motion to the fly, and the trout, catching a general impression of correct size and colouring, absorbs it, hook and all, without too nearly considering the things that belong to his peace. Taking it by and large, the fact is indisputable that the shabbiest, roughest, most dilapidated, most broken-winged fly is as likely to kill as the newest and freshest of the fly-tier's confections—provided size and colour be right. What is "right" must be the subject of further discussion. Meanwhile, I think I have established this, that in appreciation of form and proportion and detail the sight sense of the trout is defective.

III

The Invisibility of Hooks

But there is another matter in which his eyesight sometimes serves him ill. Dr. Watts—I think it was that great and good man—represented a wise old mother trout assuring her too ardent offspring that "that horrid fly is meant to hide the sharpness of the hook." It may be so, but performance, alas! often falls far short of intention, and the instances are few in which the horrid fly does anything of the sort. Indeed, a very competent school of Scottish fly dressers is all for minimum of wing and body, and the rankest exposure of the hook which is possible, so that the fly is the merest sketch, and the hook is the prominent thing. Therefore, in speculating on the vision of the trout, we have to make our account with the fact that, whether the hook be blued or brown, it does not deter trout from frequently seeking to make a meal of the artificial fly. The trout, therefore, must either fail to see the hook, or, seeing it, must ignore it. If he sees it and realizes that it is an unnatural appendage to the artificial fly, he could hardly ignore it. He must therefore either take it for a natural appendage, or for some casual, but quite irrelevant, attachment, or be so obsessed by his intentness on his food as to see only what he wants to see—namely, that combination of colour which seems to him to correspond with the natural insect in favour for the moment. It is impossible to say that he does not take the hook for some casual attachment, for all sorts of odd things float down the water with the natural fly. Yet he will not as a rule take a fly to which a weed attaches. The trout are familiar with those nasty little thin leeches which attack their own heads and bodies. Whether these ever attack floating flies I could not say, but I never saw or heard of their doing so. The balance of probability, I think, leans to the theory that the trout is so obsessed by the pressure of appetite that he only sees what he wants to see—his supposed insect prey—and ignores the hook as an irrelevant detail,* all of which goes to prove that the wily trout of the poets and journalists is—may Providence be devoutly thanked for it—really rather a stupid person.

IV

The Sense of Position

If it be true, as has been suggested, that the trout is so obsessed by the pressure of appetite that he is when feeding lost to the sense of all things connected with his food except colour and size, that would tend to account for a phenomenon which anglers at large accept with a philosophy born for the most part of ignorance, but which is a distressing problem to anglers of a more entomologically learned and conscientious type. The phenomenon is his willingness to take the winged fly under water, where winged flies are comparatively seldom found. An ultra-conscientious angler might go further and be pained

---

*This is in keeping with his being satisfied if his colour sense be satisfied and with his lack of a clear sense of form.

by his willingness to take nymphs floating high and dry above the surface, a position in which nymphs are not to be found at all in nature. But at this point the ultra-conscientious angler usually stops, and, obsessed by the appetite for catching his trout, sees only what he wishes to see, and persuades himself that the bright cock's hackles on which the artificial nymph body is held high and dry above the water really represent the much denser and duller-hued wings of the natural dun, it being generally known that the dun not infrequently stands on the points of its wings on the water.

It is a fact which no arguing can get over that the trout, whether of chalk stream or rough river, will, so frequently as to take the case out of the exceptional, take a winged fly wet and a hackle fly dry, as well as a winged fly dry and a hackle fly wet. In particular, when bulging, a trout will be so set on his subaqueous meal that he becomes almost unconscious of what is going on on the surface (and is, therefore, much less readily put down than a trout which is taking in the hatched fly), and accepts with almost equal readiness the natural nymphs and the angler's winged Greenwell's Glory, provided the colours appeal to him as right. He seems able to obliterate from the field of vision all irrelevancies such as hooks and wings, and to concentrate on the olive of the body.

There is less difficulty in accounting for his taking a hackle fly on the surface. If it represents a spinner, the effect may be right enough, but if it represents a dun, either hatched or in the nymphal stage, then it is possible that the bright cock's hackles surrounding it are the "trailing clouds of glory" with which it comes, and they may lead to an early closing about it of the shades of the prison-house which every trout carries with him, and then all is well with the angler.

If I were really spiteful, I might suggest that many of the winged floating patterns are only taken because of their resemblance to nymphs, the wings being ignored. And, truly, I could elaborate quite a pretty argument on the subject, with instances in point.

But be all that as it may, it would seem that the vision of the trout is defective in not keeping him alive to the incongruity of the winged fly under water and the hackled nymph on the surface. The only alternative explanation is that his observation, his memory, and his power of reasoning from the known to the unknown are much to seek.

V

A Problem for the Optician

I was casting a fly one sunny July day upon a shallow Berkshire brook, which, cutting its way through a boggy surface soil, babbled gaily, seldom more than eighteen inches deep, over a hard-core bed of chalk and gravel. The brook swarmed with trout, few apparently under the half-pound, and very few over the pound; and when first I arrived at the water-side the only fish taking were a few casual feeders, which picked up a miscellaneous *hors d'oeuvres* under the bushes which lined a part of one bank where the stream, being deeper, was also slower. But as I moved upstream, at every bend I came upon a new group of trout, which darted up stream and down in a great state of agitation, long before I could come within casting distance of them. After I had walked up three or four of these groups, and could see that the character of the stream for some distance ahead differed in no material wise from that part under my elbow, I returned to my starting-point and sat down on a stile to give the trout time to settle. In less than half an hour dimples here and there in the runs between the cress-beds a little way up encouraged me to try again. What a change! Fish, that half an hour before had scuttled desperately while I was yet a long way off, took no notice of me now, went on feeding gaily, and did not disdain my Olive Quill on those occasions when it was put to them right. To cut a long story short, I landed during the daytime twelve brace, retaining two over the pound limit; and going out again in the evening I landed other five brace, of which one was over the pound, and was retained.

Next day was similar in conditions, and I fished for a couple of hours in the morning, catching five brace, of which one was one and a quarter pounds, one a safe pound, and the rest went back. All the while that the fish were feeding they took no notice of me—comparatively speaking, of course—until they were hooked, when they made a fierce resistance. When they were not feeding they were wild as hawks, and scuttled over the shallows in droves while I was yet a great way off. Nothing remarkable in all this, of course—nothing that is not within the experience of all anglers for trout. The experience, I admit, is quite commonplace. It is only because of a train of thought to which it gave rise that I mention it, and mention it in detail. Were the trout so infatuated with their food that they did not care about me during the rise, or was it that, with their eyes concentrated on the nymphs and duns coming down to them, they could not see me without a special effort, or without some special cause attracting attention? If one supposed that for reasons of self-protection, or for some other sound natural cause, the eye of the trout had a wide range of focus, so that he could see—even behind him—to quite a distance out of water when not intent on his food, and that when food was toward that focus shortened to a few—perhaps a very few—inches to deal with the business in hand, would not that explain his comparative unconsciousness of the angler's presence far better than the supposition that appetite was so strong upon him as, without diminishing the acuteness of his vision, to cast out fear? It is worth thinking about.

The human eye focuses itself upon an object, and it sees that object clearly—its immediate surroundings clearly enough; but those which are not the object of attention are often blurred and impressionist in outline and effect. If the object of attention be near, the effect of distant objects is blurred and lost. Imagine a like result in the eye of a trout, and allow for a denser medium than air. While the attention is focused on the food, feet or inches off, it may well be that the mechanical effect on the lens of the eye is to blur or even to shut out altogether comparatively long-range objects, such as an angler in the rear extending forty feet or forty-five feet of line in his direction. It might even be that, with the focus of his eye shortened, a trout becomes incapable of seeing through water on one side when the light is in a particular direction, while remaining quite capable of seeing distinctly what is behind him on the other side. In earlier pages I have endeavoured to show that the vision of the trout is defective, at any rate as regards the form of the fly, while attentive to colour and size. The mouth of the trout is large, and when he takes in the fly he does not, as so many artists depict him as doing, snap it. He expands his gills so as to induce an entering current through his open mouth, which carries fly or nymph in with it. Therefore he has no need to see the detail of his food very clearly in order to take it in. May it not be that this defective near vision when concentrating on the fly is the correlative of the distortion of the eye from its more general business of keeping a watch for possible enemies?

Whether it is so or not I am not prepared to say. I am no optician; but if some angler who is an optician would make a study of this subject, and could deduce from his anatomy of the eye of the trout the truth of this matter, he might be conferring upon anglers some knowledge worth having.

VI

The Sense of Number

If the conclusion from my argument be accepted that trout have a defective sense of form, and will often take for a fly something that is either so tumbled or so differently arranged from the natural insect it is supposed to represent as to be very unlike it to the eye of man, the reader will have no difficulty in accepting the corollary conclusion that with the sense of form (and probably from the same cause) the sense of number is also at fault. Countless writers have poured scorn on the imitation theory, because the hackle of a winged fly suggests many more legs than the natural insect possesses. I suggest that the fish gets only a general effect, and that, provided the excess of hackle be not so pronounced as to spoil the general effect by producing an appearance of clotting, it will not be fatal to the fish taking the artificial fly for a natural fly.

VII

The Sense of Colour

1. A Query.

So many who have argued in print on the subject of
the colour-sense of trout have argued as if there were
only two possible alternatives—namely, that trout
must see colour as mankind see it, or else must be
wholly colour-blind. I venture to suggest that that
attitude of mind takes too little account of the wonderful variety of nature. It might well prove to be the
case that, without being colour-blind, trout are more
sensitive to some colours than to others, or they
might be wholly colour-blind to one primary colour
and keenly sensitive to others.

A person completely colour-blind sees all objects
in a neutral grey, the form and reflected light alone
distinguishing one from another.

A simple way of illustrating what I mean is to
take things in their simplest form. There are three
primary colours—violet, red, and green. All other
colours are a combination in varying proportions of
two or more of them. The simple combination of
any two of them makes the complementary colours.
Sensations of different colour are produced by rays of

light of differing wave-lengths. Now assume, for the sake of argument, that trout are sensitive to red only, and colour-blind to violet and green. Then a combined colour made up equally of violet and red would look to him precisely like a combined colour made up of red and green in equal proportions, for his eye would only accept the wave-lengths to which it was sensitive and reject the rest, thus selecting that part of the combined colour to which it was sensitive, and rejecting that part to which it was blind. And any shades made up of a combination of green and violet, in whatever proportions, without any red, provided the tone were the same, would look much the same to him.

Let us go a step further and imagine him confronted with a combination of orange and green, making a sort of dirty brown: his eye would pick out the red from the combination, and would reject the violet and green; and, the less red there was, the fainter the object would appear. Again, if he were confronted with a combination of green and pink, making another combination of a sort of brown, his eye would select the red and reject the green and violet. And the two quite different shades of brown would look practically identical to him, provided there were the same intensity of red in each. Again, if the combination were violet and orange with the same amount of red in the orange as in the other two combinations, his eye would again select the red and reject that part in those parts of the combination to which he was blind. So that this combination would again look the same to him. In fact, his only test of colour would be the extremely simple test, the degree of red in it. If that were constant all colours would look alike.

Yet one step further and imagine your trout sensitive to red and green, but entirely blind to violet. Then any combination of red and violet entirely free of green, or of green and violet entirely free of red, would be judged by the amount of red or green in it, as the case might be. But if red and green were together in any combined colour, then the fish would begin to be able to perceive distinctions.

It is unnecessary to drag the reader through the further combinations to make this point clear.

Now all this is extremely crude, and it is not put forward as suggesting an opinion that trout are blind to any one or two of the primary colours. That is not the suggestion at all. Nature is not so simple as that. But it is quite another matter to say that, because man has a highly-developed sense of colour, therefore trout, if capable of colour-sense at all, must see colour as man sees it. There are degrees of colour-consciousness in man, and it would surely not be a great stretch of imagination to conceive that trout's sensitiveness to different colours may well be different from that of man. He may be more or less sensitive to some colours, and relatively less or more sensitive to others—possibly extremely insensitive to some; and he may be sensitive to some beyond man's colour scale.

If this be conceded, merely as a basis for argument, it would certainly be found to result in trout seeing likenesses of colour where man sees differences, and perhaps differences of colour where man sees likenesses.

In a previous chapter I have, I think, made it fairly clear that trout do see likenesses where man sees differences, and differences where man sees likenesses. Is it too big a jump in reasoning to infer that there may be some variation in degree of sensitiveness to different colours between the eye of the trout and the eye of man?

But can it be doubted that if the fly dresser knew exactly the degree of the trout's sensitiveness and insensitiveness to different colours, and also knew the combinations of colour producing any particular shade for the trout, he would have gone a very long way towards solving the secrets of fatally successful trout-fly dressing?

It is, I think, beyond dispute that trout are extremely sensitive to red and are greatly attracted by it. Witness the value of a Red Tag to a fly. Living as so many do among surroundings of green weed with a diet of insects in so many shades of green, it seems unlikely that they are insensitive to green, but there are practically no blues in the trout's habitat unless you count the blue of the sky seen through the circle of vision above him. And it would not surprise me if it were proved that trout are comparatively insensitive to blues.

It may be that Sir Herbert Maxwell's famous red and blue May flies were, in fact, the one the colour of supreme attraction, the other a neutral grey.

On no point is there great divergence of opinion among anglers than on this of the power of the trout to distinguish colour; but it is only possible to reason from one's own experience, and to appeal to that of others. For the moment we are dealing with the colours suggesting current daily food, and setting aside the colours of lures which excite tyranny, rapacity, or curiosity. These latter are usually bright and stimulating, and they are rather beside the point for our argument. The colours of the nymphs, duns, and other insects which form the daily menu are in general sober, and if trout were incapable of making fairly fine distinctions of colour, it is hard to account for those frequent occasions when fly after fly is tried, seemingly like enough to the fly on the water, in vain, and finally a pattern is found which kills fish after fish. Again, on wet-fly waters, where the angler is laying a team of flies across the stream, one fly out of the three or four will be persistently selected by the trout, and if two or more anglers are using the same pattern on diverse casts they all find the same pattern selected. My own belief, for what it is worth, is that where the supply of food is moderate or small and the fish is hungry, his taste is apt to be far more catholic than on those occasions when there is a strong hatch of one or more varieties, one of which appeals most strongly to the trout. There must have been days within the experience of most of us when the water has been covered with yellow duns and small pale olives, with a sprinkling of iron-blue duns among them, and all else has been neglected in favour of the iron blue. Here it is true that the fly is quite distinct in colouring from the others on the water at the same time; but on similar occasions, when the iron blue is not to the fore, the trout will as a rule not be mixing their diet, but confining themselves to fly of one kind, and sticking to that, and that only, and letting all else go by.

So far we have been dealing with surface feeding mainly, but where the trout are bulging it is not so easy to ascertain what they are feeding on. It involves an autopsy—a messy and uncertain business at best—for it is impossible to say when and where the nymphs in the gullet were taken; one can only make an approximate guess. It is true that one generally finds one type of nymph predominating, but one often finds odd specimens of other kinds, and it may be suspected that the trout, accustomed where no rise is on to forage among celery beds and other vegetation in search of nymph and larva, shrimp and snail, is then much more catholic in his tastes than when he is busy gathering in the surface duns. If one puts down a soft muslin net among celery beds just before the rise is expected one will bring it up wriggling with larvae and nymphs of very varying dimensions and colouring, from darkest olive to something like bright dandelion and primrose. So it may easily be true that the trout when nymphing may more readily be induced to make a mistake than when feeding steadily on the surface. There it is much more important to get the right fly. And the right fly is that which the trout finds to be the right colour. It does not always seem the right colour to the angler, and so it may fairly be questioned whether the trout sees colour just as man sees it. This is a question which deserves to be pursued further, but this is not the place to pursue it.

2. A Speculation.

To set about discovering in what the difference (if it exists) of sensitiveness to colour in the eye of the trout and the eye of man consists, is an extremely difficult matter. I do not profess the anatomical or optical knowledge which would enable me to probe it scientifically. I do not know whether the problem is or ever will be soluble, whatever be the scientific advance of man. I hope it may be possible to solve it some day, if it be for the good of fly fishing as an art. In the meanwhile I may perhaps be forgiven some empirical speculations in the direction of a solution, some gropings after the truth.

It may, I think, be taken as a starting-point that, whatever be the nature of the trout's faculties of vision, they are designed to subserve his earning his living and the preservation of his species.

One starts by observing that in weedy rivers trout live in an environment of green; in gravelly or rocky rivers they live in an environment of brown. One knows from the attractiveness of the Red Tag and the Zulu that they are peculiarly sensitive to red.

In their food one finds among the duns a prevalence of greens and yellows; among the sedges reds, orange, and brown; in the Perlidæ, or willow flies, browns; and in the alder brown and plum colour. There is not, however, except very faint in the wings of duns, any great quantity of blue in the food of trout, nor does it prevail in their habitat, except in combination with yellow to make green. I am not forgetting the iron-blue dun. That is easily to be picked out as a very dark fly against the light, and not necessarily because of the blue in it. Indeed, the base colour of the iron blue, as disclosed in its spinners, is a shade of red as exemplified in the claret spinner and the Jenny spinner. The wings of duns, standing up in the air or seen spread out spent on the water, are generally very colourless, and it is known that many anglers fish hackled flies habitually in preference to winged flies.

It would not perhaps be the worst guess that could be made if one were to hazard that blue was the colour to which trout are least sensitive.

It is the colour of sky and cloud, the background against which they see their surface food.

The reference to a neutral grey recalls a greenheart rod of mine made by Farlow and painted heron-blue, and its extraordinary invisibility to the trout. Again and again I have held it over a trout lying under my bank, and have waved it to and fro without scaring him until I showed myself, and it certainly seemed as if it were of a colour to which the trout was almost insensible. I remember speculating at the time whether it was by reason of his scheme of coloration that the heron was able to get within striking distance of the fish. I afterwards had a split-cane Test rod built by Messrs. Hardy Brothers, and I got them to colour it similarly, but the varnish put a flash upon it which discounted its invisibility, and that and the fact that the colouring matter under or in the varnish added not a little to the weight of the rod led to my discontinuing the use of heron-blue colouring for my rods.

VIII

The Sense of Size

"The fuller the water the larger the fly" is a good general working rule, and so it follows that where, as in the chalk streams, the flow is steady and constant, there is seldom any occasion to increase the size of the artificial fly above the normal size of the natural. And on these streams one is liable to find that the

"On the Upper Test," from Martin Mosely, The Dry-Fly Fisherman's Entomology *(1921), shows chalk stream anglers of Skues's day on the famous stream.*

presentation of a fly above the normal in size is apt to be resented, and many experienced anglers advise a size smaller than the natural fly rather than an imitation of equal size. What, then, is the ground for the use of a fly larger than the natural upon rougher and less constant streams? The only one which suggests itself is that a full water (once it clears enough for the fly) stimulates the fish to such high spirits and such extremity of hunger, that the added size of the angler's lure, so far from giving rise to suspicion (as it would in more normal circumstances), becomes an added attraction in its promise of satisfaction of an oppressively vigorous appetite. The angler therefore may be sure that he will be wise to pay attention to this matter of size, as it is one of which, for good or for ill, the trout takes notice. It is a curious point that the wet fly may be fished a size larger than the dry representing the same insect. I record this as a matter of experience without being able to give, off my own bat, even a guess at a reason. A very skilful and observant wet-fly angler of my acquaintance says that the nymph and the creeper are larger than the winged insect.

The conclusions which I venture to submit as the sum of the foregoing arguments and inferences are that in flies purporting or intended to imitate natural insects, size and colour are the matters of consequence, and that, apart from mechanical considerations as to the structure and wearing power of the fly, shape is of very secondary consequence.

IX

Tone

One theory of some who do not believe in the colour vision of trout is that it is tone only of which they are conscious—meaning by tone, I assume, shade of colour, irrespective of what that colour may be—so

that all colours of similar shade look alike to him—
say a neutral grey as to a totally colour-blind man. It
is an attractive theory in that it might account for
cases of trout seeing likenesses between the artificial
fly and the natural fly where man sees only differences—such as the case of the Blue or Grey Quill
being taken for the pale watery dun at least as well as,
if not better than, the Little Marryat, or of the
Orange Quill being taken for the blue-winged olive
or its spinner—at dusk. It does not, however, seem to
account for cases within one's daily experience on
chalk streams where a single pattern proves fatal to
the trout after a whole series of other patterns of
apparently similar shade have been ostentatiously
ignored. It is suggested by some that trout looking
up at the fly from below always see it more or less
black against a background of sky. There may be
instances where this is approximately true, but they
must be comparatively few, and more frequent at
night than by day, and in either case only when the
fly is between the fish and the source of light. Where
the source of light is behind the fish or at either side
he will, I am convinced, see (or at any rate be in a
position to see) far more colour than the theory
under consideration would permit one to suppose.
The position is, of course, quite different where the

light is in any way in his eyes or eye. He might therefore be far less critical of a fly passing on the sunny side than on the shady side of him. The theory allows nothing for the fact that so many natural flies have bodies more or less translucent, nor for the light thrown on to the underside of their bodies by reflection of light from the surface of the water, from the bottom (brown gravel, grey chalk, or red rock), or from the often brilliant-coloured weed-beds below. Looking up from a glass-walled chamber beneath water-level at artificial trout flies floating on the surface, one certainly sees them in much more detail than the theory under consideration would suggest—to say nothing of their being enveloped in iridescent colours, an effect which may be due to their being seen through a prism of water. One sees them thus even where the body of the fly is opaque and gets its effect from reflected light; and it may be that it presents to the trout by reflected light the same effect as the semi-translucent natural fly presents by means of light partly transmitted and partly reflected. There are, of course, many artificial flies in which, by means of dubbing, or celluloid, or stained gut, or horsehair, an effect of translucency of body is obtained similar to that of the natural insect represented, and often a bit more brilliant. In such cases the trout would get the effect of transmitted as well as reflected light—and one may appeal to the experience of anglers as to the efficacy of such patterns to combat the tone theory. That theory, moreover, hardly accounts for the specially attractive effect of scarlet on the trout. It is not one with which the writer holds, and accordingly he sees no special advantage in the silhouette fly patterns advocated by that very interesting writer and skilful angler, Dr. J. C. Mottram.

X
In Dusk and Dark

The capacity of the trout for distinguishing flies in the dusk or dark has often been the subject of comment. I first noted it in September, 1888, on the Coquet, when, the August dun being up, its spinners, after looking like red-hot needles dancing in rays of the setting sun, were later on the water. I was fishing the tail of a run under trees with a team of three flies, all representing the spinner, tied on eyed hooks with gut bodies dyed a flame-coloured orange, a reddish furnace hackle, and wings from the ruddy feather of a partridge's tail. One of my three flies was winged from the portion of the partridge-tail feather which is finely freckled with black, the others from the unfreckled part of the same feather. On several evenings I found the trout invariably selected the fly with the freckled wing and entirely ignored the others. On a Norwegian lake, fishing during the short July night when the wind had dropped dead, I have found the same one of a team of flies accepted again and again while the others were ignored. On the chalk streams again, the ability of the fish to draw fine distinctions at night must have struck every observer. I recall one evening when the trout were taking the natural blue-winged olive well. I tried a Red Quill dyed orange on a No. 1 hook, after getting my solitary Orange Quill soaked and slimy through killing a brace; but the trout would have none of it—though they took the Orange Quill again when I had washed and dried it. Yet the only distinction between the two patterns was that the quill of the Orange Quill was plain condor, and in the Red Quill it was the usual ribbed peacock. It was dyed in the same dye in each case. In fact, the Red Quills had been supplied to me as Orange Quills. That was years ago, and I have the remains of the dozen still, for they have never been any good to me. Again, I recall one evening when I rose eighteen trout, all short, to a Tup's Indispensable dressed to represent a spinner

"The Test at Stockbridge," from George A. B. Dewar,
The South Country Trout Streams *(1899).*

with a ruddy colouring, and then, putting on a fly of
identical size with a body of rusty-red seal's fur, I
began to get firm rises immediately. This must have
been something more than a coincidence.

I have had it suggested to me by a distinguished
angling writer, whose opinions deserve respectful
consideration, that trout disregard colour during the
daytime, but distinguish it at night. While accepting
the latter proposition, I do not accept the former,
though I do not profess to understand how they see
colour under either condition.

It might seem bold to express the opinion that
they distinguish textures at night, seeing that they

undoubtedly take confections of feathers, silk, and fur for natural flies; but I think it clear that at times they evince at night a preference for artificial flies of one texture of body or wing rather than another, such as herl, rather than quill, or *vice versa,* as indeed they do by day. For instance, the difference between landrail and starling dyed to landrail colour is not very obvious to any but the trained eye of the fly dresser, but I have known trout reject the sedge fly winged with dyed starling and greedily accept an exactly similar pattern winged with landrail. Again, it is well known that an Iron-blue nymph hackled with the blue-black feather from the throat of a jackdaw will be accepted freely when a fly hackled with an apparently identical hackle from the crest or other part of the same bird will be contemptuously ignored. In the same way the Waterhen Bloa must be hackled with a feather from one particular row of feathers from under the waterhen's wing—the simi-larly coloured feather from the next row being useless. Other less well-known instances will be familiar to North-Country fly-fishermen. Numerous instances could no doubt be recounted where trout drew no such distinctions, for their fastidiousness is much more marked on some waters than on others. Indeed, I once fished a tributary of the Test where my host told me the only fly I need use, whatever might be on, was the Red Quill. It was an August day, with a nice rise of pale watery duns, but the trout took the Red Quill all day. Thank goodness, the trout of my length of the Itchen know enough to keep one guessing all the time.

And now comes the time to consider the upward vision of the trout.

XI

Looking Upward

At this stage I should like to consider further the theory put forward by writers well deserving of attention that the colours of flies, natural or artificial, are not distinguishable by the fish because the fly comes between the trout's eye and the light.

In order to do this effectively it will be well to get some idea first of how things look to the human eye from under water, not because the trout necessarily sees exactly in the same way, but because it is the only way in which it is possible for man to realize the lighting conditions of the under-water world. The theory above mentioned is generally supported by reference to the experiment of placing a glass dish containing water in such a position that lying on one's back one can look up through it at a floating fly. In such a position, no doubt the fly would be against the light, and it would probably appear indistinct in colouring, for one would be looking perpendicularly upwards into the light. A trout, however, seldom sees a floating fly by looking perpendicularly upwards at it. Indeed, at the moment of taking it it must be at least the distance from his eye of the tip of his neb, and while the fly is approaching the trout more or less rapidly it must be seen at an angle to the perpendicular from the trout's eye to the surface. In these conditions the trout cannot always have the fly between him and the strongest light. If the sun be low and be shining directly down-stream towards the trout, then the conditions would approximate to those of the experiment quoted, and the light would be entirely from behind the fly, and its colour, unless it be transparent, would not perhaps be readily distinguishable.

But if the sun were exactly the opposite way and were shining exactly behind the line in which the fish is swimming, would not one suppose that the approaching fly would receive enough illumination to enable the trout to apply to it such appreciation of colour as he possesses? Between this condition of things and the condition prevailing when the light is coming right down into the trout's eyes, there must be a large range of conditions in which a greater or less degree of visibility of colour would appear to be possible.

This is, of course, all upon the assumption (which may not be correct) that the trout sees as man does. His eye is adapted to the medium in which it works, and it is at least conceivable that it is so constructed as to enable him to overcome the difficulty of appreciating colour with the light behind it. It is certain that it has a faculty of choice of fly, indicating a degree of appreciation of colour, or tone, or texture in the dark or deep dusk, so that it might not want much light on the underside of the fly to enable it to appreciate its colour, tone, or texture in any direction. The light reflected from the bottom, gravel, rock, or weed, might be enough. We do not know.

I was given the privilege, some few years ago, by Dr. Francis Ward, the author of "Marvels of Fish Life," of spending some hours in his underground observation chamber built below water-level on the side of an artificial pond with plate-glass sides cutting off the water from the chamber; and with the assistance of Mr. H. T. Sheringham, the Angling Editor of the *Field,* I made some brief experiments in the direction of trying to divine how trout see the fly, whether floating or sunk.

The pond was a cement construction, lined at bottom with rock and pebble, but showing from the darkened observation chamber in one side a far side of bare cement. The water came flush with the top of the glass window. The first thing that struck me was that the whole cup of the pond seemed reflected upside down except for a little semi-circle of light just above my head, and as one looked up into the semi-circle of light it seemed as if one were gazing into a big ball of water with a little round hole of rainbow light at the top, and except at this hole the sky was cut off by a sort of mirror, like plate-glass. But the tank was full of light, reflected from the bottom and no doubt back again from the mirror made by the underside of the surface. The semi-circle, of course, indicated by its edge the margin beyond which rays from above proceeding in the direction of the observer's eye ceased to penetrate the surface. I believe that rays striking the water at an angle of more than 48 degrees to the perpendicular above the eye of the observer will be reflected back skywards and substantially do not penetrate. In the same way if one looks beyond the edge of the semi-circle—*i.e.,* outside the angle of 48 degrees—one does not see through the surface, but only sees the bottom of the tank reflected on the surface. Thus a fly floating on the surface outside the angle of 48 degrees from the perpendicular to the eye of the observer is unseen, unless it or a part of it penetrates the surface, or makes some impression on it breaking up its mirror-like smoothness. If some impression only is made, it may, and no doubt does, afford the fish some indication that something, which may be fly-food, is approaching. If it, or any part of it, breaks through the surface, then that part only which breaks through the surface becomes visible outside the angle of 48 degrees, and it is reflected against the underside of the surface. This was well illustrated by the effect produced by the gardener's birch broom being thrust into the water to sweep aside some discarded shucks which had fallen from budding trees into the water. Only that part of the broom which was put through the surface was visible, and that was duplicated by reflection. The rest, for all that could be seen of it, might as well not have existed.

But inside the semi-circle, within the angle of 48 degrees, everything floating on the surface was not only visible, it was extremely clearly visible, and was surrounded by a prismatic radiance which was more specially in evidence the nearer the fly was to the outer edge of the semi-circle. There was no difficulty about distinguishing the colours of flies on the underside or on the sides. Indeed, the effects produced were all much what I have suggested above may be the light effects where the light is behind, or at any rate not directly shining into the eye of the trout.

I blame myself for not having ascertained and recorded precisely the position of the pond and the observation chamber in relation to the points of the compass, and the relative position of the sun at the time of observation, so that I might be able to deduce with more certainty the difference in appearance of a fly with the light between it and the fish and a fly between the fish and the light. The day, however, was very overcast.

A May fly was the first subject—one tied with summer duck wings, red hackle and tail, and a brown dappled pseudo-natural body—a most effective pattern, by the way, in Southern Germany. The first thing we noticed was that, when thrown on the surface dry, the gut was not noticeable from underneath, except in the semi-circle of light, and not very noticeable then. Outside that area the fly was like the broom. No part of it could be seen, except what had broken the surface film and passed through it. Thus, one sometimes saw the hook only—more generally part of the body and the lower part of the hackle—

and we could conceive that, to a trout, a floating artificial May fly, not too dry, passing outside the transparent circle above his head, would appear at a little
distance like a nymph, only taking shape as a winged
fly when he got it within the circle of light above his
head. Beyond this there was the fact that to us the
under-water parts were duplicated by reflection. In the
rainbow semi-circle of light above the observer's head
in the pond the whole artificial May fly became not
only visible, but extraordinarily and brilliantly so. The
wings seemed coated with a spun-glass brilliance
which was most attractive. It may have been all in the
observer's eye, because it is quite conceivable that,
looking up through a triangular wedge of water, one
may have been looking through a sort of prism, which
perhaps gave the rainbow effects above referred to.

With the May fly sunk below the surface, much
of the brilliance was lost, and the gut became obvious
at once. But whether the fly was outside or within
the rainbow hole at the top, it was extremely difficult
for the observer to say that it was not on the surface,
except by deduction from the fact that it was visible,
and would not have been so outside the semi-circle
had it been floating. A sunken fly was readily visible
at quite a distance through the water, when a floating
fly at much less distance was, but for the hook, clean

out of sight. The insistence of the dry-fly angler on extreme accuracy of casting and absolute dryness of gut and fly seems, from these observations, so far as they go, to be thoroughly justified. It is also obvious why a trout which will move a long way to intercept a nymph or sunken fly is not to be tempted by a dry fly that does not come accurately over him into the circle of light above his head.

Later we sank a large Pink Wickham, and it looked dead as mutton, and with the light behind it all the golden brilliance of its body was lost. Not even in the magic semi-circle above the observer was the glitter visible, but it is conceivable that, were the fly floated over brilliant green weed in sunshine, the green of the weed might be thrown upwards on to the belly of the fly, so as to reproduce the effect of a green-bodied sedge. In the dull light which we had, the brown stone bottom sent off too little reflection to give any noticeable effect. Even as it was the body did not look black. But some silver-bodied and gold-bodied salmon flies, which were dangled over sheets of metal painted blue, green and red, took up these colours, despite the dull day, very splendidly. So there can be no doubt that the effect of colour reflected from the under-water surroundings on the body and hackle of a trout fly is a question of degree. It may be considerable. The old trout-fly dressers were well aware of the ability of hackles—especially cock's hackles—and furs to take up light and colour from one another, so as to attain unsuspected harmonies. Thus, you might take two dun cock's hackles, apparently exactly alike, and, tying one over a mole's-fur body, get a dusty grey effect, and, tying the other over a hare's-ear body, get a rusty brown effect! They also knew the value of an admixture of seal's fur or mohair in the body, in throwing up and affecting the colouring of the hackle. And I cannot help thinking that the rage for quills sacrifices a great deal that was of value—and still would be—in the dubbed body of the trout fly.

A small spent spinner—one of the then new Halford patterns—dropped on the surface showed nothing whatever, except an extremely black and obvious hook, duplicated by reflection, breaking through the surface in a tiny patch of blurred and broken light, due, no doubt, to the hackles; and when viewed in the rainbow semi-circle one could not candidly say that it looked (apart from the hackles) at all fly-like, or anything but dense and hard against the light. But my friend told me that when the spinner was floating less high on its hackles, and was in fact somewhat waterlogged, it looked very fly-like and attractive. A homemade Tup's Indispensable, tried next, had a distinct advantage over the spinner when floating. Sunk, it presented quite a nymph-like appearance, and it was quite comprehensible that a trout might come some way to fetch it. The same might be said of some seal's-fur-bodied nymphs which we also tried. In a dull, shabby way they had a lot of translucency. We next tried to fathom why a Greenwell's Glory, fished wet, should be taken at all below the surface. As my companion said, it was "a fine representation of a Greenwell's Glory," and on the surface it might have passed as a rather shabby olive. Under water it went down always with its narrow wings upright, and it may be that it is taken because the trout is too foolish to realize that it is not on the surface. Much the same might be said of a small dotterel hackle, tied Stewart-wise, with waxed primrose silk on a No. 00 hook. It might have been taken for a hatching nymph caught at a disadvantage with its wings half out, or, again, it might not, but I cannot think of anything else.

I was not below in the observation chamber to observe the effect of a floating Coch-y-bondhu made in the old style, or a Kennedy's floating Coch-y-bondhu beetle. Our last experiment with the trout fly was with a good-sized floating Sedge, but I recall nothing new or of interest about it.

I recognize that it is not safe to dogmatize or deduce very much from these very incomplete, very brief, and very imperfect observations, made by one like myself not equipped with the scientific knowledge to draw the inevitably right deductions from them, and the little which I have since observed does not take me much further. I do not know the true meaning of the structure of a trout's eye. I cannot tell what may have been the disturbing or distorting effect of the sheet of plate-glass between me and the water. And there are doubtless many other factors I have not allowed for, and I recognize that the course of experiment ought to be pursued systematically for weeks and months and years in all sorts of lights and all sorts of weather before any safe deductions can be drawn. So my readers (if any have got so far) will understand me that I am putting forward this record of my observations, not as establishing anything, but as containing perhaps some suggestions for investigation which others, more fortunately situated and better equipped than I am, may be able to follow up and verify or disprove.

XII

Looking Upward in Dusk and Dark

Under another heading we have considered the trout's vision looking upward in daylight. Let us now try and put ourselves in his place after the sun has gone down and darkness is supervening. What effect has this upon the trout?

It is a remarkable fact that, until the sun's rim dips, the evening rise does not begin. Often it does not begin then; but, though a stray fish may take a fly here and there, generally in parts when the sun shines down-stream, the evening rise proper never begins before, and it often begins directly after—immediately, that is, that the sun's direct rays are off the water. It is true that this is the time that spinners choose to come down upon the water—sometimes spent and dying, often with wings erect. But at times one sees quite enough new subimagines hatching just before sunset to bring on a rise if it were at any other time of day, and often there are many spinners then on the water. And if there be a hill, or high river bank, or a screen of trees which takes the direct sunlight off the water earlier than the hour of sunset, there one sees the evening rise accelerated. This is a fact of which the angler, desirous of making the most of his evening, may make profitable use while waiting for the general evening rise to begin. It would seem, therefore, that the diffused light reflected from the sky after sunset provides the trout with better conditions for seeing his surface prey than are afforded by the sunlight impinging directly, but at a low angle, upon the surface. The lighting may be scanty—but what there is of it strikes to a large extent straight down from the sky—and it would almost seem as if the trout could thus see better than if vision were confused by the almost horizontal rays of the setting sun. It would be interesting to see whether similar conditions prevail just before sunrise. I have never been up early enough to see. I have often observed that on a dull day, with diffused light only, the trout are much more alive to the presence of the angler on the bank, and much more cautious in their scrutiny of the artificial fly than on a bright day with full sunlight. The dull day of milk-and-watery glare makes the water look much clearer and full of light than does the bright day.

We have seen from previous investigation that trout have a strange power of drawing distinctions of colour, and perhaps of texture, in the dusk and dark, and it may be that the under-water world is then relatively better lighted for the trout than the above-water world is for man. If this were so, it would account for the trout being able to distinguish colours from underneath.

Years ago I picked up from a pedlar on Ludgate Hill a square of plate-glass mirror about five inches by five, in the hope that by means of it I might be able to get some idea of how an artificial fly looked to a trout. I placed it at the bottom of a large papier-mâché basin, and floated flies over it. But though no doubt it gave a fair idea of how a fly looked in point of shape, I soon concluded that its value from the point of view of colour was probably largely discounted by the fact that the mirror reflected on to the underside of the fly light which in quantity greatly exceeded and in quality of colour greatly differed from that which would be reflected by rock or gravel, or sand or green weed. I therefore carried the matter no further, and the mirror went the way of all mirrors.

Recently, however, a friend in the medical profession procured and sent me a laryngeal mirror, one of those little circular mirrors on a long metal bar, like those by the aid of which dentists manage to see the interiors of the hollow teeth on which they are working, while they are working on them; and he suggested that by means of the mirror I might readily see how the artificial fly looked to the trout. Though it seemed to me that this experiment must be subject to much the same objection as the former one, yet, seeing that the mirror could be adjusted to get a variety of points of view, I tried it. First I was unable to find in my house a bowl which was not white inside; so, rather than do nothing, I filled a white slop-basin with water and floated on it a pale watery Tup's Indispensable. There could be no doubt about one being able to see the entire coloration of the fly reflected in the mirror just as clearly as one could see it from above. But this may have been, and probably was, largely due to the white colour of the bowl and possibly in part to the light reflected from the mirror. I tried a Whirling Blue dun under the same conditions and with the same result, and the only good I got from the experiment was to prove the fact that, at a distance which might be measured in fractions of an inch, the mirror, if held only just under the surface, showed no part of the fly except those parts of hook and hackle which had penetrated the surface. At this stage I abandoned the experiment with the white basin, satisfied with having seen again how it might be that the deeper a trout lies the larger is the circle through which he is able to see the floating fly, and the nearer the surface he lies the smaller the circle, and that as he approaches it or it approaches him very closely he may scarcely be able to see anything of it but the impress of its feet or hackle on the surface, and thus may be blind to its incorrectness of detail, and may be satisfied with the general impression which he gained while it was farther off.

The next step was to procure coloured jars for a resumption of the investigation with the laryngeal mirror, and I selected jars of dark green and dark brown as being the colours best approximating to weed and rock, and deep down in them, in a room too far from a window for direct light from the sky to strike the surface of the water, I floated a Red Quill and a Pheasant-tail Red spinner. Putting the mirror deep under them, I saw every detail with all the clearness of detail with which I saw it looking down upon it in the open. Later on, in a corner of the Itchen in the shelter of a boathouse and a bank, I placed the mirror under some natural red spinners and pale watery duns floating spent upon the surface, and again every detail was as clear from below as it was to me looking down upon the flies from above. This test may have been vitiated by the fact that it was carried out under the open sky, so that the little mirror may have reflected upon the flies the light which made the detail clear. At any rate, up to this point I have seen nothing to prove that the trout looking up at the floating fly, natural or artificial, sees it in silhouette without colour (except, perhaps, when the fly is directly between him and a strong light), and much to lead me to think that he probably sees it, according to his capacity for appreciating colour, as clearly from below as man does from above. I consulted Dr. Francis Ward, the author of "Marvels of Fish Life," upon the subject, and he suggested the use of a trench periscope so boxed in as to exclude all possibility of the mirror reflecting back upon the underside of the fly the light of the sky, but up to the present I have not been able to give the scheme the necessary attention.

There is, however, the indisputable fact that the trout, which at dusk, in the absence of moonlight, is unable to distinguish the angler casting a short line close behind him, is able to make fine distinctions of pattern in the flies presented to him, and that fact suggests to me that the under-water region is better lighted for his vision than the air above.

PART IV

How

I
The Mouth of a Trout

"And lo, it stuck
Right in his little gill."
Dr. Watts

Among the many hundreds of trout which have been the victims of my luck or skill, I have never known one which was hooked in the gill, *pace* the good Dr. Watts. So it is not unreasonable to conclude that the indraught of water which takes the angler's fly into the trout's mouth does not, by some miracle of contrivance, project the fly against the gills by which the indrawn water is expelled.

The mouth of a trout is, relatively to his weight and length, larger than that of any, I think, of our fresh-water fishes, except perhaps that of the pike. It is serrated all round the edge with fine teeth, and the roof of the mouth and the tongue are armed with far more formidable ones. For the purposes of taking and retaining the fly I cannot conceive that these teeth are of much service. They seem better suited to the purpose of the capture of minnows and other small fry, which but for them might escape by wriggling, and I have little doubt that the escapes so often made by a too lightly held trout are often due to his using the tongue-teeth as a sort of toothpick, to extract the hook from the roof of his mouth or the side of his jaw.

If the angler in his bath makes the experiment of trying from below water to catch some small floating object on the surface, he will find it evade him again and again, pushed away by the current set up by his approaching hand, and it looks a miracle that the same thing should not occur with the trout, especially when his approach is swift. But if the feeding trout be watched as he rises to the fly, it will be noted that there is, as he opens his mouth, an expansion of the gills which carries a stream of water, and with it the insect, in with a rush. What is the process by

"The Itchen at Itchen Stoke," from George A. B. Dewar, The South Country Trout Streams *(1899).*

which, on the water being ejected through the gill, the fly, natural or artificial, is retained is not known to me. It may be an operation of the tongue, but I think not. In any case, until the water is sufficiently expelled to enable the fish to feel or taste the capture, there is necessarily an interval, which constitutes the angler's opportunity, when that fly is his artificial one, to pull the hook home. When the fish is taking larvae, or nymphs, or other subaqueous life carried by the current, the process is just the same. It is probable that if, in either case, the fish lipped the hook or the gut, there would be an instantaneous ejection of the dangerous morsel. Taste (which is, after all, a phase or development of the sense of touch) would warn him that at best the object was indigestible and unprofitable; experience might hint that it was dangerous. When trout are well on they take with a big gulp, often accompanied by a distinct "gluck" or smack of the lips; but there are days when the fly seems to be sipped in with a minimum of water through scarcely opened lips, and on such days the angler is apt to miss an abnormal proportion of rises.

This, then, being the method of the trout in feeding, one can readily see that minute accuracy of observation of the relative parts of a fly, as regards arrangement, and proportion, is not of consequence to him, except to guard him against the angler. Innumerable natural flies come down to him partially entangled in their shucks (is it possible that the bronzed hook is ever taken for an adhering shuck?), or in disarray through some misfortune or another, and all that is essential for feeding purposes is that he should take that which in size and in combination of colours is like that on which he has been feeding. Any closer noting of detail would be as much thrown away as would minute observation of the detail of each fish be thrown away in the case of a diner eating whitebait at the Carlton. Each fly is too tiny a morsel, and passes too quickly, for much leisure to be spent on inspection.

II

A Speculation in Bubbles

In the oft-repeated description of the imagined introduction of the novice to the dry-fly art, the typical classic touch in the drama is the disappearance of the dun and the single bubble floating where a moment before the dun had been. But never in all the papers and articles in which I have read this description have I seen the faintest speculation as to how the bubble comes about. Yet it may be worth while to consider the way in which it is produced.

It is true that, if one lies supine in a deep bath full of water with one's arm submerged and brings one's fingertips to the surface, like the neb of a trout taking down a fly, and then turns them sharply down under water, one may produce a bubble or bubbles—generally the latter. It will, however, be found that some degree of violence is needed to produce the effect. But when a big trout is taking flies under a bank, and sending down single bubbles at each rise, he usually seems to be taking so softly, with such a minimum of effort and such an almost imperceptible dimple, as to exclude the idea of the degree of violence necessary to produce the tell-tale bubble. Clearly the air which fills the bubble is not in the mouth of the trout as he rises. There is, however, another possible explanation. When the trout sucks in the floating fly, is it not likely that he at the same time sucks in some air with it, and that he has to expel it: that in the act of expelling the water which he draws in with the fly he also expels the air with the water in the form of the bubble which gives away the position? It is in favour of this solution, that when trout are bulging, or in softer fashion taking nymphs under water, or even spent spinners flush with the surface, one does not note the bubble. It is only when floating flies, standing up on the surface, are being absorbed that one sees it, the reason probably being that it is more likely to require a gulp of air to take down a creature standing on the water and in the air than to take anything under or even flush with and adhering to the surface. The value of this, if it could be established, is that the presence of the bubble would be a fair indication that the trout producing it was engaged in the taking of floating duns.

III

The Rise

When the angler sees a tell-tale ring upon the surface of river or lake, he is apt to say, "There is a rise." But if, when fishing, he should have his fly taken by a trout, whether under the water or at the surface, he would in recounting the incident say, if he were a Briton, "I had a rise." If an American, he would say, "I had a strike." The term "rise" is, therefore, used rather loosely—so loosely that for the purpose of considering the subject thoroughly it is desirable to start with a comprehensive definition of what it is intended to cover by the term in the course of this discussion. I propose, therefore, to use the term here, not in the sense of indicating the break in the surface caused by the movement of a trout in the act of feeding on insect life, but as covering every movement of the fish in the act of so feeding.

Now trout inhabit waters of all degrees of pace and stillness, and of all degrees of depth and shallowness. In all of them they feed on insect life; and it must be manifest to the merest tyro that differing conditions produce differing evolutions in the act of feeding. The items of insect nourishment absorbed by a trout are, in general, individually small, and, as a mere matter of instinctive natural economy, it could not pay a trout to expend in securing his prey more effort than the nourishment produced by the food would replace, or even so much, if he is to live and thrive.

From this reasoning one can see why big trout tend to feed on the natural fly less and less, and are often only to be tempted by the May fly or a big sedge. They prefer to spend their efforts in securing prey of a size which will more than repay the effort expended in securing it. From this cause the older trout are apt to become cannibals. For the same reason the trout of comparatively gentle and not too deep streams, where the fly is secured with the minimum expenditure of effort will continue to be fly-feeders till they have reached a greater size than the trout of faster streams or of deeper, slow streams or lakes, where the coarse fish and the life of the river or lake bottom present larger individual items of diet in sufficient profusion.

The trout, therefore, though a powerful and vigorous fish, may be accounted a lazy one in the sense that he persistently maintains the utmost economy of effort consistent with living and thriving, and with the satisfaction of a healthy appetite as a means to that end. He will never face a strong stream for the mere pleasure of doing so. At times he may seem to be doing so, but careful observation will generally show either that he is in dead or comparatively slow water, or that he is getting such a supply of food brought to him by the current as to compensate him for the effort. He need not be seen to break the water, for a stream of subaqueous food is being brought to him, so that the faintest turn to right or left, or upwards or downwards, enables him to field it with the minimum of exertion. Again, except to intercept another fish or to prevent the imminent escape of his prey, he will seldom swim against a strong or even moderately strong current to get food which the current would bring to him. An apparent exception, which may at times be noted at the beginning of a rise, of a trout, generally a big one, cruising upstream and feeding as he goes, is not a real exception; for that trout, if he be watched, will be found to have been proceeding from his hole or shelter to a corner where he may expect a concentrated stream of fly-food to be brought to him by the current.

Thus, in still or slow waters which do not bring a sufficient supply of food quickly enough, trout either feed upon the bottom, or in mid-water, or near the surface, but in either case must cruise to find the food which is not brought to them.

Again, in eddies of swift or comparatively swift streams, where during the rise little fleets of becalmed duns or other insects lie almost motionless, trout will be observed cruising slowly along, picking one here and another there, and luring the angler ever upward till suddenly the rising ceases, and the trout is seen ready to resume his beat at the bottom of the eddy, which he will do unless scared by the angler or his rod.

Thus it appears that in different conditions trout rise in a variety of ways, and the observation one hears made that one has to strike more rapidly to hook the trout of this river than the trout of such and such another river only means that the conditions of the former river exact a quicker rise than those of the latter. This may in part be due to the fact that the trout of the former river run smaller than those of the latter, as, the larger the trout, the slower, other things being equal, is his rise.

With these preliminary considerations before us, let us proceed to examine the action of trout rising under varying conditions. A good start may be made in the High Street of Winchester, where below the Town Hall a fast but narrow stream runs from a culvert between brick walls alongside the Public Gardens. There one may generally see several brace of vigorous trout, but it will be rare to see one break the surface in feeding. Yet that they are well fed is evident. The stream is shallow, but they lie as deep as they can, and the swifter part of the water passes overhead. To test how they feed, however, make a few little rolls of new bread and throw them in. In a moment the fish is in the current. He does not rush to meet the bread. He merely adjusts his fins, and the current swings the roll to his mouth, where it is sucked in by the expansion of his gills. In just the same way the trout of a glassy glide, just below and flush with a carrier which prevents them from seeing many natural insects on the surface, may at the time of a strong rise be seen busily stemming the strong current and moving slightly to left or right to meet and take in the ascending nymph, or whatever it may be, brought down by the stream. If, however, the food supply brought down be scanty the fish may be seen lying in holes and behind or in front of rocks and weed patches, and either inert or picking food off the weeds, or lifting for a moment into the current to annex something, and dropping back again to a position of shelter which deflects the main weight of the current from them.

Looking over a stone bridge one will often see a good trout just above a pier or pillar which divides the current, where he is in a sort of cushion of slow water which makes the least demand on his energies, but leaves him free to move rapidly into the stream to either side to intercept subaqueous food. In such a position he but rarely comes up to the surface, whether for a natural or an artificial fly.

Another position of great advantage for a trout is the tail of a pool. There he can lie low in comparatively shallow water with the weight of the current passing over him, and the whole of the food coming down from the pool concentrated into the neck, as it were, of the bottle, so that with a minimum of exertion he can take toll.

Similar positions of vantage are to be found in rough streams where the current pours between two rocks, and the trout can swing out from shelter into the current to snatch his fly and be back again.

In all these instances the trout will take far more food below than at the surface. Let us suppose, however, that lying deep he sees a fly coming down the stream on the surface. He is lying horizontally in the water. He shifts the plane of his fins, the current sends him upward, and thereupon his body, instead of meeting the current end-on as hitherto, receives some of the force of the current on its underside, and, exposing thus a larger surface to the force of the current, he tends to drop back down-stream, as his mouth comes up to meet the fly, with the body at times almost perpendicular to the surface. Then, opening his mouth, our fish by means of an expansion of his gills induces a small current of water, carrying the fly in with it. It is at this stage that he

makes the only real effort, beyond the initial alter-
ation of the plane of his fins, in the whole process.
He has to turn down to regain his station, and this
requires a vigorous turn of the whole body in order
to overcome the upward thrust of the current, and to
convert what was an upward movement into a downward one. It is this turn downwards, with its brisk
curving of the body and sharp thrust of the tail, that
produces that surface effect which, in the case of a
fish feeding under these conditions, is commonly
known as "the rise." And it follows that the faster the
water the more vigorous that turn must be, though a
swirling water will disguise and carry away its effect
much more than will a smooth stream.

The structure of the vertebral column of the
trout does not permit of much movement in any
direction, except the lateral. Therefore the downward
turn, where it cannot by reason of the force of the
stream be effected by means of the fin planes alone,
has to be effected by a sideways twist, the flash of
which (as "the little brown wink under water") has so
often afforded to the wet-fly angler the one hint that
it is time for him to tighten on his fish. Chalk and
limestone streams generally present numerous points
of vantage where the stream, with or without the aid
of the wind, concentrates a steady sequence of sur-

face food, and it is at such points that trout will be poised, either in shelter, ready to ascend, if the stream be strong, or near the surface, if the stream be gentle. These points are generally under banks or at the tails of weeds from which the ascending nymphs are shed, and these are accordingly the places watched by anglers. And it will often be found that, even when there is no rise of fly, a small Sedge fly floated over such a place will bring up a trout which, perhaps for fear of being displaced by a rival, is hanging on to his place of vantage.

But, alike in chalk streams and in other streams, there are slow lengths where the surface food does not come rapidly enough to permit of a fish waiting for it. In these, therefore, he will be cruising, either at the surface or in midwater or deep, with an upward eye on the surface and the intervening water. If he be cruising at the surface he will sip the fly gently with a minimum of effort. If, however, he be lying at mid-water or deep and comes up to the fly, he will do so with a slash or a "strike," as if he feared to be inter-cepted by a rival; but he will gather most of his food in mid-water or at bottom. In these conditions it may well be understood that a big fly of a beetle type, well sunk and drawn slowly or in short darts, may often prove far more attractive than a floater.

The Ramsbury water on the upper Kennet, rented for a term by Mr. F. M. Halford and his friends, is in its lower lengths, at any rate above the Mill (locally called "pounds"), nearly all of the mill-head character, and that no doubt accounts for the failure of the most able management, in spite of lavish expenditure on stocking and on destruction of enemies, to convert it into a free-rising water. It may therefore be judged that such waters present a legitimate case, not only for the wet fly, but for a dragging wet fly.

It is the stream of moderate pace and comparatively even flow, therefore, that is suitable for the dry fly. The upstream wet fly fished without drag is suitable to that type and to faster and rougher streams, and the dragging wet fly may be used at both ends of the scale.

My lake-fishing experience has been so slight as to disentitle me to say much about it. But it seems to me that the same principles which apply to the rise of trout in slow or still waters in rivers must be found in action in the case of trout in lakes. In my limited experience all the big fish have seemed to be found as a general rule on shelving ledges where the water ran from six to ten feet deep, and they lie or cruise at the bottom and come up with a slash at the fly. Often the only rises seen are those which are evoked by the angler's flies; and it would seem that the main food was at the bottom, but that surface food, if sufficiently attractive, was not despised. That would seem to account for the fact that lake flies are dressed larger than corresponding river flies, for I suppose experience has proved that the trout is unwilling to come up far for a small fly.

Occasionally, however, when the wind has dropped, trout may be seen making small dimples on the surface of a lake; and I recall one such occasion when I picked up in a morning six brace of fish approaching a pound average, fishing a long line ending with a Greenwell's Glory, double-dressed on gut with No. 00 hooks, and cast behind the eye of the fish, which again and again turned and took it with the greatest innocence.

So far in my observations I have dealt with the fish taking the fly as food, and not from any other motive, such as curiosity, tyranny, jealousy, rapacity, or pugnacity (when the action is generally, even in fast water, more in the nature of a strike than a rise); and I have not dealt with the nature of the indications of the rise afforded to the fisherman under differing circumstances—for to do that it is essential to consider not only the position and convenience of the trout and the nature of the water, but also the character and condition or life stage of the food which the trout is taking. For it will be found that different classes and conditions of food are taken by trout in different ways. And all the movements described are, moreover, further conditioned by the season of the year, the health and vigour of the fish, and his ability to contend with fast waters, and his hunger or sportiveness, and his appetite or preference for special varieties of food; also by the state, temperature, and colour of the water, and the character of the light in relation to the fish's position. Sometimes in streams trout are so full of vigour that they throw themselves right out of the water, taking in the fly in the upward rush, and come down head first into the water to resume position. The effect of the character and condition of the food of the trout upon the action of the rise and its indications, and the clues which rises of different character accordingly afford the angler as to the food which is being taken, must be the subject of a separate chapter.

IV

Assorted Rises

A close study of the form of the rise may often give the observant angler a clue, otherwise lacking, to the type of fly which the trout is taking, and to the stage and condition in which he is taking it.

So far the present writer has found in angling literature, whether permanent or ephemeral, no systematic attempt to differentiate the varying forms of the rise of trout. There has been little evidence of any general consciousness of distinctions more precise than that between bulging, or under-water taking, and surface feeding, and in this respect this deponent makes no pretence of having been more acute than his fellows. It has, however, for some time past been growing upon him that, as no phenomenon in nature but has its cause, so the varying forms of rise, which every angler with the fly must have observed, are all dictated by the nature of things. It is conceived that there are several things which naturally influence the character of the rise, these being the position of the trout in the water, his degree of confidence or appetite, the smoothness or roughness of the surface, the pace of the current, and the nature and stage of the fly-food being taken.

In the examination into these matters which follows, the writer makes no claim to be authoritative or exhaustive, but he hopes to awake among the keener minds an interest in the questions discussed which may lead to some pronouncement which shall be at once exhaustive and sound in all its conclusions.

The chalk streams and rivers of quiet and even flow obviously afford greater facilities for observing the phenomena of rises than do streams less clear or of more turbulent habit, and it is from the chalk streams that one can most easily acquire the bulk of the data which may be applied, with the necessary qualifications, to the solution of similar questions on other streams. The illustrations here given will, therefore, in general be found to be taken, unless otherwise stated, from chalk streams and chalk-stream fishing, and it is not proposed to deal here with the effect of rapid current on the various types of taking.

Every chalk-stream fisherman, however much or little he may have thought about the subject, will recognize that there are a great many forms of rise. It is now proposed to consider some of these, and to try and ascertain what clue they severally give to the food the fish is taking.

Analyzing broadly, the insect taken will be either—(1) poised on the surface; (2) flush with the surface, as being either spent or entangled by wetting of the wings, or in the earlier stage of the process of hatching; or (3) subaqueous.

The best known and the most obvious rise is that in which the trout takes the floating dun or upwinged spinner. It is the foundation rise of dry-fly theory and practice, and it is to this, with the spent spinner rise thrown in, that the dry-fly purist would, in theory at any rate, confine the angler. But, as a matter of fact, this super-surface taking forms only a small part of the evidence of a trout's feeding known as the rise, and it is often supremely difficult to determine whether a given rise or series of rises be at food super-aqueous, flush, or subaqueous. Much of the floating fly-food of the trout is very small and hard to detect on the surface, and it requires some close watching to say whether it be sipped from above, or at, or just under, the surface. Thus it must come about that many a would-be dry-fly purist has spent busy hours presenting a floating fly (and at times with a measure of success) to trout which are only taking subaqueous food. From this painful and humiliating position there is little chance of escape unless the purist makes a point of actually seeing the fly on the surface taken by the fish (and preferably identifying the insect) before he ventures a cast. Not a great many purists are always so perfectly pure as all that.

Assuming, however, that the insect be seen coming down to where the fish is seen or known to be lying in wait, the trout comes up from a greater or less depth, with more or less diversion to right or left, and, with more or less confidence or eagerness, and, with a smack, a suck, or a sip, takes down the fly. The smack involves some exposure of the neb and a considerable ring in the water; the suck shows the neb under a small hump of water which never ceases to cover the fish. The sip does not expose the neb at all. A fish coming from a depth and turning down again naturally makes more of a swirl, from the energy expended in the movement of turning down again, than does a fish hovering just below the surface and merely putting up a nose. The size of the fly also makes a difference. The tiniest insects are sipped, the larger ones are taken down with much more of a swirl. The rise to the blue-winged olive at night (and by day, too) is indicated by quite a large kidney-shaped whorl; and the large dark olive of spring and late autumn is taken in a similar way. The degree of eagerness of the fish also has an effect on the size of the swirl he makes in taking. The fondness of the trout for the iron-blue dun, for instance, leads him to take it with an agitation which betrays him to the observant angler as feeding on the iron-blue dun or its nymph, though no iron-blue dun may have been observed on the surface or in the air. Naturally, too, the trout makes less of a ring when he can be confident of securing his fly than when he has to hurry to secure it ere it be whipped off the water by wind or its natural tendency to take flight.

Where duns are floating in eddies one often sees trout sailing gently under and sipping them softly. Occasionally in these positions one sees a succession of head-and-tail rises—first the neb appears and descends, then the back fin, and then the upper portion of the tail fin. It is my belief that this in general indicates that the trout is taking duns which through accident or defective hatching are lying spent or on their sides on the surface. The same type of rise in the open stream may generally, especially in the morning, before the dun hatch, and in the evening, be taken to indicate that the trout are taking spent spinners. In the eddies and over weed-beds, however, when no fly is visible on the surface, it may mean that the trout is taking nymphs, just in the film of the surface, about to hatch, or, it may be, swarming for refuge in eddies after a weed-cutting; and these may be nymphs of duns or gnats. In these circumstances nymphs seem to be taken with a quiet deliberation very different from the swashing eagerness with which the bulger swirls to meet his under-water prey. Very often, however, in streams the trout will be nymphing for hours together with just the same quiet deliberation and with just as little excitement as when taking floating duns; and, as on these occasions there is no head-and-tail rise, the angler is usually immensely puzzled to make out on what they are feeding. The writer does not profess to have worked out any reason why nymphs should be taken on one occasion with the head-and-tail rise and on another with an action apparently differing in no appreciable respect from the ordinary rise to floating duns. The nearest thing to a clue he has been able to observe is that while spent spinners are taken with the head-and-tail rise, floating upwinged spinners are absorbed, especially if small, with a soft suck which spreads a ring so thin and creating so little disturbance as to be scarcely visible in the dusk or the moonlight, while within its circle the water looks like a little pool of fine creaming lines whorling towards a pinhead hole in its centre. Again, occasionally on a windy day one sees a head-and-tail rise in quite rough water. The inclination therefore is to suspect that the trout is taking an insect blown over or caught by the waves with just the action with which he takes a spent spinner or a drowned dun in the eddies, and to deduce that the head-and-tail rise is to a quarry at the surface with no chance of escape, and to make the further deduction that, when nymphs are being taken thus, they are in some stage or condition where they have no chance of escape, and that where they are taken with what looks like an ordinary rise they are capable of some, but not a great, degree of activity, and may be below the film of the surface. Then there is, of course, bulging properly so called, where the fish move to and fro to intercept the nymphs carried down by the current. Here in general the indication of the rise is the swirl of the fish as it turns after capturing its prey. There is also the rise to hatching caddis, such as the grannom—having an appearance much like bulging; the rise to the running sedge—something of a slash; the rise to tiny midges and curses, which may be an example of the ordinary rise to surface food if the insect be perfect, or of subaqueous taking if the insect be yet unhatched.

Of the rises of cruising trout in still or extremely slow water it is not necessary to add anything, except to say that at times they partake of the character of the slash and at times of the sip.

Of the rise to snails spoken of by Mr. Halford in one of his works, the present writer has had no experience. Summarizing briefly the types of rise we appear to have at least the following:

Over-Surface Rises.

Ordinary rise to floating dun or upwinged spinner and its variants, namely:

Big rise with kidney-shaped double whorl to large floating dun (such as blue-winged olive or its spinner).

Sucking rise to medium-sized floating flies.

Sipping rise to smallest floating duns, spinners, and midges, and

The slash—most commonly to running sedge, or to flies on slow water.

In addition to which there is the plunge where an eager fish comes almost entirely out of water and takes the fly either as he leaves the water or as his head re-enters.

On the Surface or Flush Rises.

Head-and-tail rises to wet duns or spent spinners or nymphs of duns or gnats suspended inert in the surface film.

Subaqueous Rises.

Bulging to nymphs.

Bulging to hatching caddis flies, such as the
    grannom.

Nymphing in eddies ⎫
                    ⎬ to mobile nymphs.
Nymphing in streams ⎭

There are doubtless other types which a more
observant eye would be able to distinguish, and there
must be many among the large body of fishers with
the fly who are well qualified to indicate them.

V

"Fausse Montée"

There is one form of rise which I have not dealt with,
to which, indeed, it is difficult to give precise desig-
nation. Speaking generally, when one sees the surface
broken one says, "There is a rise," and one means
that the surface is broken by the emerging or almost
emerging neb of a trout. But the rise I am here
speaking of is quite other than that. True, there is a
boil on the surface, but it is not an indication that
the trout is there. On the contrary, it is an indication
that he is gone. And, if he has taken the fly, any hope
of hooking him that is based on striking when the

boil is seen is likely to be vain. It will be too late, probably much too late. This form of rise is much commoner in fast, fairly deep water than in water that is slow or smooth. And when the angler finds that he is apparently getting, and certainly missing, rise after rise, he may suspect that what he is really getting is this kind of false rise, and he should, if possible, seek a position where the light falls so as to enable him to see through the surface the turn of the fish under water, and strike at that instead of at the following surface indication.

How fallacious that indication can be I saw very clearly one sunny June morning a few years back on the Kennet. I had put my rod together for a day's May-fly fishing on a beautiful length of that river, and I was waiting on a bridge above which a lovely clear shallow deepened and narrowed towards the arch. In the eye of the stream—a nice eighteen or twenty yard cast upstream—a yellow trout of near two pounds, and obviously in prime condition, lay rather deep, yet not in that glued-to-the-bottom way which rendered it hopeless to attempt to get him. There was, in fact, an air of suppressed energy and eagerness about him which tempted me to stretch over him the summer duck straddlebug which was ready attached to my cast. The fly lit beyond him, but a yard or more too much to the left. But he came at it with a flash, took a scare, turned, and was gone—three or more yards to the right of his original position; and as he came into the straight, all that way away, a huge boil on the surface surrounded and took under my fly. It was the effect of the vigorous slash he made in his turn away from the fly that only materialized on the surface when the trout was well away from it. It was obviously no good to strike, but if the light conditions had not enabled me to see the whole process quite clearly, I might have struck under the impression that I had had a fine rise and have gone in the belief that the fish had risen "short," or that I had mistimed my stroke—and have found any explanation but the true one.

I think it will often prove that when fish are rising what is called short, whether they take the submerged fly or baulk at it, as did the trout in the incident described above, what is seen is no true rise in which the fly is taken, but the belated after-effect of the trout's turn away under water coming to the surface. This turn may vary enormously in its degree of violence, and the gentler it is the better the angler's hope that the fly has been taken and that he may pull in his iron.

VI

The Moment

As Captain Cuttle is recorded to have remarked, "The point of these observations lies in the application of them." I propose, therefore, to consider the rise at the artificial fly, and to examine its indications as guides to the angler telling him when to strike.

There is, of course, no mystery about the taking of the floating fly. Provided the angler is certain that it is *his* fly that is taken, and not a natural fly an inch or more away, he has only to strike more or less rapidly according to the size of his fish. Matters are often nearly as simple for the wet-fly fisherman if the trout comes up to his fly with a swirl, but he has to remember that if his fly be well sunk he must be very quick or he may be too late, for the swirl is often (as shown above) an indication not that the trout is there, but that he is gone. That is why in a rough river a wet fly fished upstream should be fished on a short line with most of it out of water, so that the trout turning down may if possible be felt, or at any rate that there may be no loss of time in pulling home when the flash of the turn is observed. But often the trout takes so far below the surface, or with so little motion, that there is no swirl or break on the surface to indicate that he has taken. Then the opportunity may be missed unless some other hint be noted by the watchful angler. On chalk streams or smooth placid streams such indications may be found in the draw of the partially floating gut, in the flash of the turn (but this is comparatively rarely seen), or in the appearance of a faint hump on the surface, often accompanied by a tiny central eddy caused by the suction with which the trout has drawn in the fly.

Sometimes the entire process can be seen, though the fly be invisible, and then the angler will be wise if he tightens at the least motion of the fish to left or right, or at the opening and closing of his mouth, or, if the cast has fallen wide, then at the moment the fish is seen to turn back. It is surprising how often he will be found to have collected the fly. I have seen a trout let an artificial fly of the nymph type go past him, turn and follow it for several yards, and, striking as he turned upstream again, have found him fast.

PART V

What

I
Flies as Food

A general survey of the circumstances, stages, and conditions in which the insects which serve the trout as food may be preferably simulated or represented may not be amiss.

The larvæ of the Ephemeridæ have been classed as digging larvæ (of which the May fly larva is an example), flat larvæ (of which the larva of the March brown, clinging to the bottom and hiding under stones, is the most obvious), swimming larvæ, and crawling larvæ.

The digging larvæ are hidden from the trout until as nymphs they crawl up into the weeds and let themselves go into the current preparatory to hatching out as winged flies. This, then, is the only sub-aqueous stage in which they are exposed to the trout and can legitimately be simulated or suggested by the fly-fisherman. In the winged stages they are surface flies either floating with upright wings or flat with wings outspread, damaged, or spent or dipping on the surface if egg-laying.

The flat larvæ, of which the March brown is the most prominent example, can seldom in normal times be seen by the trout, since they hide under stones and seldom venture out till the time comes for their ascent to the surface to hatch out. Probably when there is a spate which tumbles over the stones, these larvæ are exposed and carried down-stream, and the trout get an unwonted good chance at them, so that they are not as unknown to the fish as the digging larvæ. At the time of ascent to the surface for hatching the trout get their real chance at them, and it is in this subaqueous stage, rather than in the stage of subimagines, that the fish feed on them most ravenously. The hatches occur in flushes, and it probably pays the fish better to slash the ascending nymph (which they can see farther than they can see the floating subimago) than to await the subimago passing almost vertically overhead.

PLATE XVI.

MAYFLY  (*Ephemera danica*)

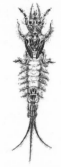

Nymph Male x 3.

Nymph Female x 3.

Though Halford provided beautiful illustrations of nymphs, like these mayflies, in his books, he maintained that imitation of them by fly fishers was doomed to failure. Skues proved otherwise. From Frederic Halford, Dry-Fly Fishing in Theory and Practice *(1889).*

The stages, therefore, in which the Ephemeridæ which have flat larvæ are legitimately to be imitated are the ascending nymphal stage and the winged stages, either floating or flush with the surface.

The swimming larvæ are obviously much more familiar to the trout. Living in vegetation or roaming over stones and gravel they are easily routed out by the trout. A familiar example of this is to be seen when the trout are tailing. Then larvæ, nymphs and shrimps are bustled out of the weeds, and are captured in the open by the fish. Then, again, at the period of ascent to hatch, these nymphs are exposed in mid-water and near the surface, and are swung down by the current to the waiting fish. An imitation nymph or larva will at times take a tailing trout, but, generally speaking, the stage in which an imitation has its legitimate chance of success is at the time of ascent, or any other time (such as weed-cutting) when the larvæ or nymphs are in open water exposed to the fish. The wriggling action of its swimming cannot, of course, be reproduced in the artificial fly, but when the swimming larva, like the other larvæ, comes up to hatch it is practically quiescent.

The crawling larvæ have a way of hiding snuggled under a thin layer of sand or mud, so as to be practically invisible. It follows that they must frequent quiet waters. Yet when spates occur they are no doubt washed out of their shelters and become a prey to the trout. They too, again, have an exposed stage when they ascend to hatch out as winged flies; and it is in these exposed stages that the imitation nymph or larva has its proper chance of success. Obviously the nymphs or larvæ cannot be imitated either on the bottom or in the weeds.

The winged insect will be taken hatching or hatched, floating cocked, or caught and disabled, and again in the spinner stage, floating cocked, or disabled, or spent, or, again, dipping to lay her eggs.

There are said to be cases where the female spinner "creeps down into the water (enclosed within a film of air with her wings collapsed so as to overlie the abdomen, and with her setæ closed together) to lay her eggs upon the underside of stones." I have never seen such a happening, but it is quoted from no less an authority than the Rev. A. E. Eaton, and must unquestionably be in accordance with the facts.

The net result, therefore, as regards the Ephemeridæ is that effective representation of them for fly-fishing purposes is as larvæ or nymphs, when in open water, and in the winged stages.

Then there is the willow-fly or stone-fly series (Perlidæ), which in the subaqueous stages live on the bottom among stones; and though in those stages they are no doubt avidly taken by the trout when the trout can get at them, they do not in those stages lend themselves to representation on a fly hook, and they are seldom in mid-water. They can, therefore, only be usefully simulated in the perfect or winged form.

There are also the caddis or case flies (Phryganidæ), which again, with the exception of the grannom, do not lend themselves to imitation, representation, or suggestion otherwise than in the perfect or winged form.

The grub crawling on the bottom in its sheath of stones or sticks or sand is no doubt frequently eaten by the trout, but does not, either in form or habitat, lend itself to representation by the fly dresser. It might be that occasionally the ascending pupa about to hatch into the perfect fly could be approximately reproduced. Indeed, the grannom is more often taken by the trout when ascending to hatch out than as a perfect fly, and a brown partridge hackle with a green silk or wool body is readily accepted as a substitute, but the ascending pupæ of other case flies are not so easy to reproduce.

There is the alder, sometimes confused with a case fly, which spends its larval stage in the mud, crawls ashore and pupates in the earth; and, though it frequents the water-side, it only drops on the water, much in the same way as a land fly, as a casualty. In the larval form, however, it would not be badly represented by a Honey-dun Bumble dressed with a palish Tup's Indispensable body; and I once had a fly, so dressed, torn to pieces by eager May trout in Germany.

There are also the gnats which breed freely in stagnant or slow water, and are taken in the subaqueous as well as the perfect and winged stage, though seldom imitated by anglers in the subaqueous stages. Finally, there are various small midges and beetles.

The land flies which get on to the water are less important. They are all in the nature of casualties, and comprise ants (of which trout are inordinately fond), sundry flies of the house-fly and blow-fly type, the oak fly or downlooker, and sundry crane flies, etc.

I do not purpose to go into the entomology of the subject, since that has been adequately dealt with elsewhere.

It follows, however, that the Ephemeridæ, the gnats and some beetles, and possibly the alder, are the only flies which have subaqueous stages calling for representation by the fly dresser. The perfect stages of all the classes of insects named may be dressed to be fished either dry or semi-submerged, or even, so foolish at times is our quarry, definitely submerged.

I think, however, it should be the ideal of the sportsman angler to take his trout, where he can do so, by means of imitations, representations, or suggestions of its natural food presented in the conditions in which the trout is feeding on it.

It is very usual to find writers declaring that to attempt to represent or suggest the natural fly with sufficient exactness to deceive the fish is absurd, and that one fly will do as well as another, provided the size and something of the modesty of nature be observed. I can only say that thirty-seven years of fishing of chalk streams have convinced me that this is not true of them, and that the trout will, more frequently than not, refuse any but one pattern which for the time being appears to them (though it is not always obvious to the angler why it does so) to be the natural fly on which for the moment they are feeding. For instance, it is not very clear why, when the blue-winged olive is rising at night, and the trout are taking it on the surface, a large Orange Quill on a No. 1 or even a No. 2 hook is accepted readily by them, but a large Red Quill of the same size, dyed or undyed, will either be utterly ignored or will put down the trout. The only difference is the colour of the quill. Other instances of unlike likenesses being taken are the taking of the Blue Quill when the pale watery dun is on, the Gold-ribbed Hare's ear when the large spring medium olive dun is hatching, and the Whirling Blue dun for the big autumn olive.

Often, of course, the insistence of the fish is upon closer likenesses. Yet it is my constant experience that on such waters a minute variation makes the difference between failure and success.

For instance, in July, 1919, the July dun was coming up freely on the Itchen, and I was introducing a guest to the water. He put up a fly which to all appearance was a close imitation. Dark starling wings, yellow silk body ribbed with fine gold wire, and greenish-yellow olive hackle and whisk. He was an excellent fisherman, and he spent a full quarter of an hour over a vigorous trout, never putting him down or scaring him. Out of my experience I had made him tender of a pattern of July dun, which differed from his only in having the body silk clothed with pale blue heron herl, dyed the same colour as the silk, a dirty greenish-yellow olive, but he had refused with the remark that his fly was "near enough." After a while he said to me: "Well, give him a chance at your fly, since you think it better." The first time my fly covered the trout he had it, and my friend netted out a nice two pound six ounce trout. He then accepted another fly similarly tied, and putting it on gut the next two fish he tried directly he covered them.

I have had too many similar experiences to have any doubt about the matter.

Of course, the Itchen is a river which breeds and maintains a large quantity of fly-food. In rough rivers where fly food is scarce I can understand that the fish will often rise at any fly or any suggestion of a fly which comes over them. But even there, when there is a rise or fall of an acceptable species of fly, I have known occasions when the trout refused everything but a fairly satisfactory representation of that fly. For instance, on the Coquet one afternoon, seeing that there was a heavy fall of small spinners, I put on a solitary fly which I had dressed the previous day to imitate the same spinner, and I caught no less than eight-and-thirty trout with it, while a much more experienced rough-water fisherman, fishing with me on the other side of the same water and using three or four flies, one of them a wool-bodied Red spinner, but not true to shade, took three trout only. I am therefore convinced that what I call "appropriate representation" rather than exact imitation is seldom thrown away.

Every rule has its exception, and the exception is the occasion when the hatch or fall of natural fly is so copious that unless your fly has the luck to fall so near to the trout as to be the absolute next to be taken it is in competition with too many natural flies to invite selection. On such an occasion there should be something special about your fly to attract the trout's attention from the stream of natural insects.

II

Fly Dressing as an Art

I imagine that no art has ever been learned from books; fly dressing is no exception. As a mere mechanical art it can be learned in the workshop or at the fly-dressing table. There, from teaching and example, the student may acquire with practice a certain knack and deftness. But when he has acquired these it is far too soon to imagine himself a master of the art.

Many writers have attempted to teach it in their books by verbal description and by illustration, but apart from the fact that most of them leave unexplained a whole series of details of each process, which seem to them from habit to be so simple and obvious as not to require explanation, there seem to be none who go to the real root of the matter, and tell the student what he is or should be aiming at when he sets out to dress an artificial fly. In saying this I have not forgotten Cutcliffe and his "Trout Fishing in Rapid Streams." In that work, one of the soundest and cleverest in the whole range of fly-dressing literature, the author does propound, in language which lacks nothing in clearness and sincerity, a system of dressing and fishing the artificial fly as a lure. But that is only one, and far from the most important aspect of fly dressing and fly fishing; and when he deals with fly dressing from the imitative, representative, or suggestive side, he does so in a very perfunctory manner; for, for the streams of Devon to which his fishing was confined, that was not a side of the subject to which he attached much importance.

Most, if not all, of the other writers who have dealt with the subject have dealt with it locally and almost entirely as a mechanical art. While saying this (and I hope I am doing no author an injustice) I should like to make it clear that I have never read one of them and attempted the method he describes without learning something from him, and no method portrayed has proved entirely without merit.

Still, the writer has yet to come who will treat the art of trout-fly dressing as a whole, and will make clear to the learner the aims, objects, and advantages of the varying styles and methods adapted to varying conditions of brook, stream, river, and lake, and the processes by which they can be achieved.

The first stage must, I suggest, be the adoption of a clear terminology as an aid to clear thinking. For instance, most of the writers above referred to tell us that the natural fly must be "imitated"—and then they are quite likely to teach you how to dress a straddlebug or a palmer—and it is more than probable that in most cases by imitation they mean "representation" or "suggestion." Even those distinctions are insufficient. Imitation may mean imitation of life, of activity, of colour, and size. It may be obtained by transmitted or reflected light where the colour of the natural fly is reflected or transmitted. And these things are equally true of the artificial fly that is a representation or a suggestion of the natural fly.

III

Imitation, Representation, Suggestion

It is a common and a just observation that the best artificial fly bears but a poor resemblance to the natural fly which it is supposed to stand for. But, for all that, artificial flies dressed to imitate, to represent, or to suggest natural flies do take trout, and take them in such conditions that no unprejudiced angler can doubt that they are taken for their natural proto-types. This suggests defective vision on the part of the trout, and this question of vision and the nature and extent of the defect are examined elsewhere. At this stage it is sufficient to indicate the distinction to be drawn between artificial flies which are imitations, representations, and suggestions respectively of the natural insect.

Where, as for instance in the case of the Olive Quill or the Iron-blue dun, a determined effort is made to reproduce the natural insect in colour, shape, and attitude, the artificial fly may be called an imitation. It is of little consequence whether the effect be got by reflected or transmitted light. A less ambitious effort may be called a representation, while a pattern so sketchy as just to give the effect of a tumbled specimen (as, for instance, a dotterel hackle, or light snipe and yellow for a pale watery dun), may be called a suggestion.

Every artificial trout fly is necessarily a compro-mise. It has to carry a hook; to float or to sink; to be durable; to be attractive:

(a) by appealing to hunger or appetite; or

(b) by exciting curiosity, rage, rapacity, pugnacity, or jealousy.

It appeals to hunger or appetite by suggesting an insect either living, or newly drowned, or otherwise dead, in one of its aerial or subaqueous stages, or a shrimp, or (as Dr. Mottram will have it) a small fish.

Such insects may be suggested by shape; by colour; by carriage; by shape and colour; by action; by action and shape; by carriage and shape; by action and colour; by action, shape, and colour; or by carriage, shape, and colour.

The shape cannot be precise because of the hook, and because of the action of the water on feathers, and because, in the case of a floating fly, of the refractive operation of light passing from air into water.

The colour may be suggested by translucency (or transmission), by reflection, or by both.

Action may be suggested by motion in or on the water, or by position on the surface, and by such a use of hackle as to suggest a buzzing action.

The imitation may be Impressionist, Cubist, Futurist, Post-Impressionist, Pre-Raphaelite, or caricature. The commonest is caricature. It therefore catches most fish.

IV

Styles of Fly Dressing

The angler who has fished with the fly in different parts of the country cannot fail to have noted the extraordinarily differing ways in which the same natural fly is imitated, represented, or suggested in different parts of the country and for different rivers and streams.

As nothing of any permanence is without reason, it must be inferred that these differences correspond to differences in the conditions under which fly fishing is pursued in streams of different classes.

In Plate I. I have reproduced a series of patterns of the same fly—the large dark spring olive or blue dun—dressed according to methods prevailing in different parts.

Fig. 1 represents an attempt at what is styled, for lack of a better term, "exact imitation." It purports to represent the natural fly sitting up cocked on the water in the attitude in which it may commonly be seen on the clear chalk streams of the South. It has wings (double dressed) and legs, body and tails; and the colours of the different parts purport to correspond with those of the natural fly. It is fished in conditions in which, by reason of the clearness and

HAMPSHIRE

DERBYSHIRE

YORKSHIRE

USK

TEME

THE
COMMONPLACE

DEVON

TWEED

CLYDE

TUMMEL

*"The Blue Dun, as rendered in ten different schools,"
Plate I from Skues's* The Way of a Trout with a Fly, *showed ten distinct interpretations of one fly pattern as it was preferred on different British waters.*

slow pace of the water, the trout has time for a good look at the fly ere it takes it. Fig. 1*a* is a Derbyshire dressing from the hands of Mr. C. A. Hassam, of the Fly Fishers' Club—than whom no more exquisite artist in trout flies, whether amateur or professional, has ever come within my ken. The wings are single dressed and the whole fly a model of lightness and delicacy.

Fig. 2 represents the same fly as dressed for the tumbling Yorkshire and North-Country brooks and rivers. It is dressed with a fur body, which, when wet, is remarkably transparent and lets through, while it darkens and accentuates, the olive colouring of the waxed silk with which the fly is tied, and the tumbled hackle from the waterhen (moorhen) suggests the tumbled, dilapidated state in which a fly whose wings have been caught by the current might be whirled down-stream in such waters. If used as a dropper, fished upstream and across, this type of pattern with its mobile wings may well constitute an effective suggestion of a fly struggling with its difficulties upon the surface. All the Yorkshire and North of England patterns seem to be dressed upon this theory. Both these types of fly are meant to be fished upstream, or up and across. Fig. 3 is a dressing from the Usk. The Usk is a broad, solid river, where, I imagine, the bulk of the fishing is to be done by casting across stream. Here the theory appears to be that the artificial fly is a sketch. Note the slight shred of wing, the slim body, the slight but active hackle. Fig. 4 is a dressing of the fly intended to be fished downstream, or rather across and down, in such solid streams as the Teme. It has, therefore, what is described as a good entry; that is to say, a shape which is calculated to create the least unnatural disturbance through its breasting the current or swinging across it. It is to stand hard wear, so the wings are rolled into a single solid pad.

Fig. 5 is a single-winged pattern—*i.e.,* a pattern dressed with only one thickness of wing fibre to represent each wing of the natural fly—and in a variety of quality it is perhaps the commonest and least rational of all the types of fly dressing. Fig. 6 is a Devonshire pattern, dressed with sharp, bright, dancing hackles, probably intended to suggest a struggling nymph rather than the hatched winged fly.

Fig. 7 is a rolled-winged pattern with upright wings akin to the Greenwell's Glory. It is one of the few winged patterns of the Northern English counties and the South of Scotland, and its upright split wings will either enable it to go down-stream almost afloat like the natural fly, or, if it be drawn under, it will be whirled about in a way to suggest considerable life and activity. It is suitable for upstream fishing—even in chalk streams.

Fig. 8 is a type of fly affected by the fly fishers of the Clyde and its tributaries. It is extremely sketchy, but as I have never fished, or even seen, the waters where it is used I am unable to do more than guess at the theory of its operation. It appears somewhat akin to the Tweed type.

Even sketchier is the type of pattern illustrated in Fig. 9, but I have known Scottish burn fishers fill bumping creels with just such simple patterns busked before setting out with a mere wisp of feather for wing, a tiny hen hackle pulled from a fowl caught for the purpose, a few inches of tying silk, and perhaps at times a tiny pinch of wool from coat or cap for the body.

Then there are Stewart's patterns (illustrated in "The Practical Angler"). Of these the winged flies are much like the Teme flies, No. 4, but, fished upstream and across as droppers, are drawn down by the current ahead of the gut cast head upstream, while the hackled type are just soft hackled palmers which, while of the sober colours of the water insects, must really attract by reason of the mobility of the hackle fibres presenting an appearance of a struggling creature.

All these methods have their merits and all deserve study; for the fly fisherman who is also a fly dresser can be none the worse for being able to adapt his methods to the type of water he is fishing or going to fish in.

The number of ways in which flies can be tied is incredible. There are hardly two books which lay down identical methods unless one is a crib from the other. And of all the methods in which I have experimented, from Walton downwards, I have never come across one which had nothing to recommend it, and I should be glad to be master of them all.

V

Kick

This is a quality which every hackled wet fly, for us in rough water, should invariably have. Without it, it is a dead thing; with it, it is alive and struggling; and the fly which is alive and struggling has a fascination for the trout which no dead thing has. How is this quality to be attained? It is a very simple matter. Finish behind the hackle.

Suppose you are tying an Orange Partridge. You have whipped on the gut, tied in the floss, whipped to the shoulder, wound on the orange floss, whipped down the end, cut away the waste. You then take your brown partridge hackle, and placing it face downwards on top of the hook, with the stump towards the bend, you whip it down with two turns towards the head; then, whipping over the hook and back to the feather, you form the head. Then you take two turns over the butt, and, taking the centre of the hackle in your pliers, you wind at most two turns of the hackle and secure the end with one turn of the silk. Then you pull all the fibres forward over the head, and finish with a whip-finish tight up behind the hackle, and break off the waste. You then soak the whip-finish with celluloid varnish (celluloid dissolved in amyl acetate or acetone), push back the hackle over the bend and varnish the head, and your fly is complete. The turns of silk behind the hackle makes each fibre sit up and stand out, and the fly has kick, and it will improve rather than deteriorate with use. Hackles with good natural resilience are, of course, essential.

VI

Ex Mortuâ Manu

For centuries, more than most anglers suspect, we have in the matter of fly dressing been in bondage to the past. The dead hand has been heavy on us. To the newcomer to fly dressing the taking of a trout with the artificial fly seems such a miracle that he is apt to attribute some special virtue to the confection of fur and feather which has done the feat, and he falls to studying the fathers of fly dressing either directly from their works or second-hand through modern pundits, or the experts who derive their knowledge and experience either from the same sources or from the experts before them similarly instructed. Thus the body of angling lore on the subject of artificial flies is almost entirely empirical and traditional, and as every new blunder is carefully enshrined in work after work, it is tainted with every kind of long-perpetuated error and prejudice, and is distant indeed from the natural sources from which it should have directly sprung.

I have described the trout as "rather a stupid person," and, with an irony more biting than I guessed at the time I wrote, I thanked the powers that had made him so, for otherwise man would be unable to catch him with the fly. I did not at the time mean that angler man was something more than "rather a stupid person," but I say now that if the trout took as long to learn the things that belong to his taking as angler man has done, the word "rather" would be an entirely inadequate qualification for the opprobrious adjective. I speak for myself as for the rest of my craft, from Dame Juliana to the present day. Our faculty for misobserving and for misapprehending the most obvious evidence of our senses would put the most stupid trout to shame. The most caustic phrases of "A Scottish Flyfisher" would be quite too weak to convey any idea of the wrong-headed density of the whole string of writers of fly fishing from A to Z, not excluding the present scribe. From the word "go" fly dressers have built their flies upon the assumption that the winged fly, as seen in the air, is the food of the trout. For generations anglers have fished these winged flies under the surface, because they found the trout would take them there, and it was difficult to make them float. All sorts of ingenious and fanciful theories were conceived to account for the taking of winged flies under water. It took a peasant, whose entire education cost, if his preface may be believed, no more than thirty shillings,* to put first on record—though not without some natural errors of observation—that the trout takes the insect at the bottom, and as it ascends to the surface, as well as on the surface, but even he did not advocate imitating it in the subaqueous stages. It took nearly fifty years more to bring us our "Detached Badger," with his autopsies proving that the vast bulk of the food of the trout was subaqueous; that, as he puts it somewhere (I quote from memory), the under-water feeding is the beef and mutton, the floating fly is caviare to the trout, and he authoritatively squelched in Chapter VII. of "Dry-Fly Fishing" the idea that larvæ or nymphs could be successfully imitated. Hence his demonstration that chalk-stream fish could only be taken with caviare. It took twenty years more to bring me to the definite conclusion that the wet fly had a big future on chalk streams. And it took the droughty summer of 1911 (with scarce a natural dun or spinner on the surface day by day, yet with trout after trout breaking the surface as it fed in all respects as if it were taking floaters, and every trout's gullet containing nymphs and larvæ only) to lead me to experiment systematically with nymphs really imitat-

---

*John Younger, "River Angling," 1840.

ing the natural insect, and to prove that, not with-
standing the weight of authority to the contrary, the
artificial nymph will kill, and kill well, when the
trout are taking natural nymphs, or even merely not
exclusively occupied with surface food.

Now to those who prefer to catch their trout
with caviare only, I have nothing to say except that it
restricts their chances, and it seems a dull game com-
pared with that of catching them by simulation of
what they are feeding on at the time. It is, however,
at least a comprehensible theory, like barring the
anchor stroke in billiard matches. But to anglers on
wet-fly rivers, and to those chalk-stream anglers not
exclusively devoted to caviare, I would ask: Has not
the time come when the under-water fly should be
habitually presented not only under water like a
nymph, but as an effective imitation of a nymph? I
am aware that a book called "Fly Fishing: Some New
Arts and Mysteries" (Dr. J. C. Mottram) has set out
an interesting method of nymph fishing. I do not
wish to be understood as disparaging his flies or his
methods in any way, as I have never tried them. In
theory they seem to me to have the defects of rigid-
ity, density, and dulness of colouring, and a tendency
to fall heavily when cast, by reason of absence of
hackle. Moreover, they are used dragging. In practice

these matters may be of no consequence. My own
very encouraging experiments have in the main been
made with dubbed bodies containing more or less
bright seal's fur ribbed with gold wire or silver wire
(thus being full of light), and with just enough short
soft hackle to help to break the fall of the hook on
the water. But whatever method of dressing is
adopted, I, at least, urge the systematic and general
working out of a logical system of imitating the natural insect in its natural surroundings. This does not
eliminate the winged fly altogether. It can be fished
dry or when the trout are taking the natural fly on
the surface, though even then I incline to think that
the nymph will frequently be preferred. A new
Ronalds is called for to classify and illustrate the suc-
cessive series of nymphs and larvæ for the benefit of
anglers. Let him stand forth!

But even without our nymphal Ronalds let us try
and see what can be done by the application of the
sheer light of common sense. Let us suppose that all
the lore of centuries is cancelled out, and the angler
sitting down to construct, without reference to the
past, a system of trout-fly dressing. What would he
evolve?

He would first, I conceive, ascertain what
appetites or emotions lead a trout to take the artifi-

cial fly, and he would conclude that they were (1) hunger, (2) caprice or wantonness, (3) curiosity, and (4) tyranny or rapacity. For the purpose of exciting caprice, curiosity, or rapacity, he would evolve the fancy fly, and that might not be unlike some of the more conspicuous artificial flies of the present day, either brightly coloured or active in motion of its parts, or both. For the representations of insects appealing to hunger, and occasionally to caprice or wantonness, he would have to make a first-hand study of the food of the trout when freshly taken. He would net a series of trout at the middle or end of a rise, and analyze the insect contents of their stomachs. If, then, he found—as he would find—that 95 per cent. of the Ephemeridæ there to be found had been intercepted before their wings had emerged, it is safe to assume that he would not give the numerous varieties of nymph the go-by without seeing whether it were not in fact possible to reproduce them on a hook with sufficient exactitude to induce the trout to take hold. It is not suggested that he might not also evolve the floating fly for use on special occasions, but I venture to think it would take a place quite secondary to the nymph, if once the initial difficulty of imitating the nymph were surmounted. He would ascertain that during the period of preparation for the rise these nymphs were floating at large in considerable numbers, and were legitimate subjects for imitation. Not so the larval or pupal stages of the Phryganidæ and the Perlidæ, which, hiding in their cases or lurking under stones, do not, at any stage short of the perfect insect, lend themselves to imitation for the purposes of the artificial fly. The larvæ of the diptera on which the trout feed are in general too infrequent in streams or (like the perfect insects) too small to lend themselves to the purposes of the fly fisherman. Assuming, therefore, that the modern angler determined to discard these types of fly, which, either by their dragging motion or by the brilliancy or challenge of their appearance, excited the curiosity or tyranny or pugnacity of the trout, he would find himself practically confined to the floating fly and the larvæ or nymphs of the Ephemeridæ.

He could not, of course, deny that artificial flies, dressed by the lights hitherto vouchsafed to us, have caught trout in the past, or that they will continue to do so in the future. He would probably recognize that on some, perhaps on many, waters the appeal to curiosity, tyranny, or rapacity which they present affords a better chance than the appeal to appetite which the floating fly and the larval or nymphal imitation presents, and that some waters are unsuited to the floating fly. But I think he would have to admit that for an appeal resting upon appetite alone the floating dry fly, the flush with the surface tumbled floating fly, the dipping egg-layer, and the larval or nymphal imitations are the only strictly legitimate lures, and that the floating ephemera must be imitated either in the dun stage, dry with cocked wings, or spent and semi-submerged with soft dun hackles, or in the spinner stage floating, or semi-submerged with bright cock's hackles to represent the wings. He would recognize that on the surface, whether floating or semi-submerged, all fly wings and most fly bodies present to an eye looking up to them a certain degree of translucency. He would infer that to produce that effect of translucency upon the eye of the trout he would have to use materials which are either themselves translucent or which produce by reflected light the effect of translucency, like some quills in certain lights. But as dubbing will transmit light from whatever quarter, whereas quills will only reflect it if looked at from the proper point of view, he will infer that dubbings of suitable colours have advantages over quills. He will realize that the vision of the trout is not identical with that of man, and if he be a skilled optician he may deduce what that difference is, and how it affects the game. With the nymphal or larval imitation, he will see that translucency is even more important than in the case of the winged fly, and that dubbing has the advantage of quickly absorbing water and sinking his fly. This is, I think, as far as common sense, unassisted by experience on the riverside, would take him. But think of the advance. All the unnatural horde of so-called imitations of natural flies which are used under conditions in which no natural insect is ever seen, would be relegated to the true category of lures, and the angler whose business it is to take the feeding trout with the simulacrum of what he is feeding on would know what he was about, and if he chose to use any of the abominations of the past, he, at least, would do so with open eyes. At last he would be a free man, escaped from the bondage of the past. *Ex mortuâ manu, libera nos Domine.*

PART VI

Bafflement

No comfort comes of all our strife,
And from our grasp the meaning slips.
The Sphinx sits at the gates of Life
With the old question on her lips.

We have successes, and build upon them profound and far-reaching theories—to have them shattered into smithereens on the very next experience.

Hold we fall to rise, are baffled to fight better,
Sleep to wake.

And as we dwell, we living things, on our isle of terror and under the imminent hand of death, God forbid it should be man the created, the reasoner, the wise in his own eyes—God forbid it should be man that wearies in well-doing, that despairs of unrewarded effort, or utters the language of complaint. Let it be enough for faith that the whole creation groans in mortal frailty, strives with unconquerable constancy: surely not all in vain.

I conclude this section of my book with a sense of bafflement, fully aware that my speculations are mere speculations and inconclusive in result. It may be that, just as man is a creature of three dimensions, and not constructed to comprehend the matters of the fourth dimension, to say nothing of the *n* dimensions, plus and minus, extending beyond or comprehending the three in which he dwells, so man is intended never to solve the mystery of the difference between the eyesight of man and that of the trout. Be that as it may, it is beyond me, and I have come to a time of life when I cannot hope to add much to what little I have so far learned. Such as that is, however, I dedicate it to my brother fishers with the fly, in the hope that it may lead to further advances in the not too distant future, and that in the meantime it may be of some help to those who seek improvement in the theory and practice of the art of trout-fly dressing and of fishing with the fly.

SUGGESTIONS FOR
ADDITIONAL READING

The best additional reading about Skues is of course his own books. They aren't all easy to come by, though most have appeared in reprints at some point, and you can easily enough track them down at the websites of various booksellers. During his life, he published *Minor Tactics of the Chalkstream* (1910), *The Way of a Trout with a Fly* (1921), *Side-Lines, Side-Lights and Reflections* (1932), and *Nymph Fishing for Chalk Stream Trout* (1939). But various capable editors have gathered his many other writings in a series of posthumous books, including *Silk, Fur and Feather* (1950), *Itchen Memories* (1951), *Angling Letters of G. E. M. Skues*, edited by C. F. Walker (1956), and *G. E. M. Skues: The Way of a Man with a Trout*, edited by T. D. Overfield (1977). A fine larger sampler of his writings is *The Essential G. E. M. Skues* (1998), edited by Kenneth Robson.

For more on Skues's place in angling history, Overfield and Robson provide a lot of background in the above books, and a good additional start can be made in the following books.

Arnold Gingrich. *The Fishing in Print*. New York: Winchester Press, 1974.

Tony Hayter. *F. M. Halford and the Dry-Fly Revolution*. London: Robert Hale, 2002.

Andrew Herd. *The Fly*. Ellesmere, Shropshire: The Medlar Press, 2001.

Terry Lawton. *Nymph Fishing, A History of the Art and Practice*. Mechanicsburg, Pennsylvania: Stackpole Books, 2005.

Paul Schullery. *The Rise: Streamside Observations on Trout, Flies, and Fly Fishing*. Mechanicsburg, Pennsylvania: Stackpole Books, 2006.

Ernest Schwiebert. *Nymphs*. New York: Winchester Press, 1973.

ALSO IN THE SERIES

*Theodore Gordon is one of American angling's
freshest and most original voices, and his trout-fishing
tales and lessons are rich with the adventure and
awe that come from a lifetime of inspired
engagement with nature.*

Theodore Gordon on Trout
$16.95, hardcover, 4 x 6, 160 pages,
27 b/w illustrations

Thaddeus Norris's American Angler's Book *was regarded as the foremost reference work well into the twentieth century, and Norris is still affectionately evoked for his amazing breadth of knowledge, his friendly sense of humor, and his extraordinary grasp not only of how to catch fish but why we anglers are so passionate about doing so.*

Norris on Trout Fishing
$16.95, hardcover, 4 x 6, 144 pages,
20 b/w illustrations